PEOPLE OR PENGUINS
The Case for Optimal Pollution

PEOPLE OR PENGUINS;

The Case for Optimal Pollution

WILLIAM F. BAXTER

COLUMBIA UNIVERSITY PRESS
New York and London   1974

Library of Congress Cataloging in Publication Data

Baxter, William F   1929-
  People or penguins; the case for optimal pollution.

  1. Environmental policy. 2. Environmental
protection. 3. Pollution. I. Title.
HC79.E5B38   301.31   74-6102
ISBN 0-231-03820-8
ISBN 0-231-03821-6 (pbk.)

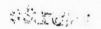

Contents

PEOPLE OR PENGUINS
The Case for Optimal Pollution

1

A "Good" Environment: Just One
of the Set of Human Objectives

I start with the modest proposition that, in
dealing with pollution, or indeed with any problem, it is
helpful to know what one is attempting to accomplish.
Agreement on how and whether to pursue a particular
objective, such as pollution control, is not possible
unless some more general objective has been
identified and stated with reasonable precision. We
talk loosely of having clean air and clean water, of
preserving our wilderness areas, and so forth. But
none of these is a sufficiently general objective: each

is more accurately viewed as a means rather than as an end.

With regard to clean air, for example, one may ask, "how clean?" and "what does clean mean?" It is even reasonable to ask, "why have clean air?" Each of these questions is an implicit demand that a more general community goal be stated—a goal sufficiently general in its scope and enjoying sufficiently general assent among the community of actors that such "why" questions no longer seem admissible with respect to that goal.

If, for example, one states as a goal the proposition that "every person should be free to do whatever he wishes in contexts where his actions do not interfere with the interests of other human beings," the speaker is unlikely to be met with a response of "why." The goal may be criticized as uncertain in its implications or difficult to implement, but it is so basic a tenet of our civilization—it reflects a cultural value so broadly shared, at least in the abstract—that the question "why" is seen as impertinent or imponderable or both.

I do not mean to suggest that everyone would agree with the "spheres of freedom" objective just stated. Still less do I mean to suggest that a society could subscribe to four or five such general objectives that would be adequate in their coverage to serve as testing criteria by which all other disagreements might be measured. One difficulty in the attempt to construct such a list is that each new goal added will conflict, in certain applications, with each prior goal listed; and thus each goal serves as a limited qualification on prior goals.

Without any expectation of obtaining unanimous consent to them, let me set forth four goals that I generally use as ultimate testing criteria in attempting to frame solutions to problems of human organization. My position regarding pollution stems from these four criteria. If the criteria appeal to you and any part of what appears hereafter does not, our disagreement will have a helpful focus: which of us is correct, analytically, in supposing that his position on pollution would better serve these general goals. If the criteria do not seem acceptable to you, then it is to be expected that our more particular judgments will differ, and the task will then be yours to identify the basic set of criteria upon which your particular judgments rest.

My criteria are as follows:

1. The spheres of freedom criterion stated above.

2. Waste is a bad thing. The dominant feature of human existence is scarcity—our available resources, our aggregate labors, and our skill in employing both have always been, and will continue for some time to be, inadequate to yield to every man all the tangible and intangible satisfactions he would like to have. Hence, none of those resources, or labors, or skills, should be wasted—that is, employed so as to yield

less than they might yield in human satisfactions.

3. Every human being should be regarded as an end rather than as a means to be used for the betterment of another. Each should be afforded dignity and regarded as having an absolute claim to an evenhanded application of such rules as the community may adopt for its governance.

4. Both the incentive and the opportunity to improve his share of satisfactions should be preserved to every individual. Preservation of incentive is dictated by the "no-waste" criterion and enjoins against the continuous, totally egalitarian redistribution of satisfactions, or wealth; but subject to that constraint, everyone should receive, by continuous redistribution if necessary, some minimal share of aggregate wealth so as to avoid a level of privation from which the opportunity to improve his situation becomes illusory.

The relationship of these highly general goals to the more specific environmental issues at hand may not be readily apparent, and I am not yet ready to demonstrate their pervasive implications. But let me give one indication of their implications. Recently scientists have informed us that use of DDT in food production is causing damage to the penguin population. For the present purposes let us accept that assertion as an indisputable scientific fact. The scientific fact is often asserted as if the correct implication—that we must stop agricultural use of DDT—followed from the mere statement of the fact of penguin damage. But plainly it does not follow if my criteria are employed.

My criteria are oriented to people, not penguins. Damage to penguins, or sugar pines, or geological marvels is, without more, simply irrelevant. One must go further, by my criteria, and say: Penguins are important because people enjoy seeing them walk about rocks; and furthermore, the well-being of people would be less impaired by halting use of DDT than by giving up penguins. In short, my observations about environmental problems will be people-oriented, as are my criteria. I have no interest in preserving penguins for their own sake.

It may be said by way of objection to this position, that it is very selfish of people to act as if each person represented one unit of importance and nothing else was of any importance. It is undeniably selfish. Nevertheless I think it is the only tenable starting place for analysis for several reasons. First, no other position corresponds to the way most people really think and act—i.e., corresponds to reality.

Second, this attitude does not portend any massive destruction of nonhuman flora and fauna, for people depend on them in many obvious ways, and they will be preserved because and to the degree that humans do depend on them.

Third, what is good for humans is, in many respects, good for penguins and pine trees—clean air for example. So that humans are, in these respects, surrogates for plant and animal life.

Fourth, I do not know how we could administer any other system. Our decisions are either private or collective. Insofar as Mr. Jones is free to act privately, he may give such preferences as he wishes to other forms of life: he may feed birds in winter and do with less himself, and he may even decline to resist an advancing polar bear on the ground that the bear's appetite is more important than those portions of himself that the bear may choose to eat. In short my basic premise does not rule out private altruism to competing life-forms. It does rule out, however, Mr. Jones' inclination to feed Mr. Smith to the bear, however hungry the bear, however despicable Mr. Smith.

Insofar as we act collectively on the other hand, only humans can be afforded an opportunity to participate in the collective decisions. Penguins cannot vote now and are unlikely subjects for the franchise— pine trees more unlikely still. Again each individual is free to cast his vote so as to benefit sugar pines if that is his inclination. But many of the more extreme assertions that one hears from some conservationists amount to tacit assertions that they are specially appointed representatives of sugar pines, and hence that their preferences should be weighted more heavily than the preferences of other humans who do not enjoy equal rapport with "nature." The simplistic assertion that agricultural use of DDT must stop at once because it is harmful to penguins is of that type.

Fifth, if polar bears or pine trees or penguins, like men, are to be regarded as ends rather than means, if they are to count in our calculus of social organization, someone must tell me how much each one counts, and someone must tell me how these life-forms are to be permitted to express their preferences, for I do not know either answer. If the anser is that certain people are to hold their proxies, then I want to know how those proxy-holders are to be selected: self-appointment does not seem workable to me.

Sixth, and by way of summary of all the foregoing, let me point out that the set of environmental issues under discussion—although they raise very complex technical questions of how to achieve any objective—ultimately raise a normative question: what *ought* we to do. Questions of *ought* are unique to the human mind and world—they are meaningless as applied to a nonhuman situation.

I reject the proposition that we *ought* to respect the "balance of nature" or to "preserve the environment" unless the reason for doing so, express or implied, is the benefit of man.

I reject the idea that there is a "right" or "morally correct" state of nature to which we should return. The word "nature" has no normative connotation. Was it "right" or "wrong" for the earth's crust to heave in contortion and create mountains and seas? Was it "right" for the first amphibian to crawl up out of the primordial ooze? Was it "wrong" for plants to repro-

duce themselves and alter the atmospheric composition in favor of oxygen? For animals to alter the
atmosphere in favor of carbon dioxide both by breath-
ing oxygen and eating plants? No answers can be
given to these questions because they are meaningless questions.

All this may seem obvious to the point of being
tedious, but much of the present controversy over
environment and pollution rests on tacit normative
assumptions about just such nonnormative phenomena: that it is "wrong" to impair penguins with
DDT, but not to slaughter cattle for prime rib roasts.
That it is wrong to kill stands of sugar pines with
industrial fumes, but not to cut sugar pines and build
housing for the poor. Every man is entitled to his own
preferred definition of Walden Pond, but there is no
definition that has any moral superiority over another,
except by reference to the selfish needs of the human
race.

From the fact that there is no normative definition
of the natural state, it follows that there is no normative
definition of clean air or pure water—hence no definition of polluted air—or of pollution—except by reference to the needs of man. The "right" composition of
the atmosphere is one which has some dust in it and
some lead in it and some hydrogen sulfide in it—just
those amounts that attend a sensibly organized society thoughtfully and knowledgeably pursuing the
greatest possible satisfaction for its human members.

The first and most fundamental step toward solution of our environmental problems is a clear recognition that our objective is not pure air or water but rather some optimal state of pollution. That step immediately suggests the question: How do we define and attain the level of pollution that will yield the maximum possible amount of human satifaction?

Low levels of pollution contribute to human satisfaction but so do food and shelter and education and music. To attain ever lower levels of pollution, we must pay the cost of having less of these other things. I contrast that view of the cost of pollution control with the more popular statement that pollution control will "cost" very large numbers of dollars. The popular statement is true in some senses, false in others; sorting out the true and false senses is of some importance. The first step in that sorting process is to achieve a clear understanding of the difference between dollars and resources. Resources are the wealth of our nation; dollars are merely claim checks upon those resources. Resources are of vital importance; dollars are comparatively trivial.

Four categories of resources are sufficient for our purposes: At any given time a nation, or a planet if you prefer, has a stock of labor, of technological skill, of capital goods, and of natural resources (such as mineral deposits, timber, water, land, etc.). These resources can be used in various combinations to yield goods and services of all kinds—in some limited quantity. The quantity will be larger if they are combined efficiently, smaller if combined inefficiently. But in either event the resource stock is limited, the goods and services that they can be made to yield are limited; even the most efficient use of them will yield less than our population, in the aggregate, would like to have.

If one considers building a new dam, it is appropriate to say that it will be costly in the sense that it will require x hours of labor, y tons of steel and concrete, and z amount of capital goods. If these resources are devoted to the dam, then they cannot be used to build hospitals, fishing rods, schools, or electric can openers. That is the meaningful sense in which the dam is costly.

Quite apart from the very important question of how wisely we can combine our resources to produce goods and services, is the very different question of how they get distributed—who gets how many goods? Dollars constitute the claim checks which are distributed among people and which control their share of national output. Dollars are nearly valueless pieces of paper except to the extent that they do represent claim checks to some fraction of the output of goods and services. Viewed as claim checks, all the dollars outstanding during any period of time are worth, in the aggregate, the goods and services that are available to be claimed with them during that period—neither more nor less.

It is far easier to increase the supply of dollars than to increase the production of goods and services —printing dollars is easy. But printing more dollars doesn't help because each dollar then simply becomes a claim to fewer goods, i.e., becomes worth less.

The point is this: many people fall into error upon hearing the statement that the decision to build a dam, or to clean up a river, will cost $X million. It is regrettably easy to say: "It's only money. This is a wealthy country, and we have lots of money." But you cannot build a dam or clean a river with $X million—unless you also have a match, you can't even make a fire. One builds a dam or cleans a river by diverting labor and steel and trucks and factories from making one kind of goods to making another. The cost in dollars is merely a shorthand way of describing the extent of the diversion necessary. If we build a dam for $X million, then we must recognize that we will have $X million less housing and food and medical care and electric can openers as a result.

Similarly, the costs of controlling pollution are best expressed in terms of the other goods we will have to give up to do the job. This is not to say the job should not be done. Badly as we need more housing, more medical care, and more can openers, and more symphony orchestras, we could do with somewhat less of them, in my judgment at least, in exchange for somewhat cleaner air and rivers. But that is the nature of the trade-off, and analysis of the problem is advanced if that unpleasant reality is kept in mind. Once the trade-off relationship is clearly perceived, it is possible to state in a very general way what the optimal level of pollution is. I would state it as follows:

A "Good" Environment
12

People enjoy watching penguins. They enjoy relatively clean air and smog-free vistas. Their health is improved by relatively clean water and air. Each of these benefits is a type of good or service. As a society we would be well advised to give up one washing machine if the resources that would have gone into that washing machine can yield greater human satisfaction when diverted into pollution control. We should give up one hospital if the resources thereby freed would yield more human satisfaction when devoted to elimination of noise in our cities. And so on, trade-off by trade-off, we should divert our productive capacities from the production of existing goods and services to the production of a cleaner, quieter, more pastoral nation up to—and no further than—the point at which we value more highly the next washing machine or hospital that we would have to do without than we value the next unit of environmental improvement that the diverted resources would create.

Now this proposition seems to me unassailable but so general and abstract as to be unhelpful—at least unadministerable in the form stated. It assumes we can measure in some way the incremental units of human satisfaction yielded by very different types of goods. The proposition must remain a pious abstraction until I can explain how this measurement process can occur. In subsequent chapters I will attempt to show that we can do this—in some contexts with great precision and in other contexts only by rough approximation. But I insist that the proposition stated describes the result for which we should be striving—and again, that it is always useful to know what your target is even if your weapons are too crude to score a bull's eye.

2

The Effective Use of Resources and the "Problem of the Commons"

All of our environmental problems are, in essence, specific instances of a problem of great familiarity: How can we arrange our society so as to make most effective use of our resources? I use the term "resources" broadly and mean to include within it not only all the physical components of our planet earth —its waters, its air envelope, its minerals, and its tillable soils—but also human energies, acquired human skills, which is to say technology, and finally our existing stock of tools—manufacturing plants and other forms of capital investment. There is some particular deployment of those resources which, at any point in time, will yield a larger aggregate quantity of goods and services than any other deployment; and a major goal of social organization is and should be to approximate that optimum deployment as closely as possible.

That this should be a major goal is sometimes questioned: it is popular today to decry as crass and materialistic the suggestion that we should be attempting to maximize our production of goods and services. But that popular pastime is at best a semantic quibble and is more often an exercise in building up and then knocking down straw men. The statement is only materialistic if one arbitrarily defines goods and services in a materialistic way, and I do not. I will use the terms "goods" and "services" to connote the entire range of physical and ethereal things from which any particular individual may draw sustenance or satisfaction; and that includes automobiles and can openers, schools and medical care, sonnets and symphonies, clean air, sparkling trout streams, and unspoiled vistas. If one defines goods and services in this very broad way, it is almost tautological to say that we should strive to have as many or as much, in some combination, as our skills and natural resources will permit. But that definition of the term is the most useful—perhaps the only useful definition. Basically the reason I insist on including all of that infinite variety of sources of human satisfactions within a single rubric is because it is true with respect to any one of

them that the amounts currently available to be enjoyed are not fixed by factors beyond our control. We
can have more of any one if we wish, but generally
speaking we can have more of any one only if we are
content to do with somewhat less of another.

It is comparatively easy for us as a human society
to alter the *composition* of this aggregate basket of
goods and services—to consume more of one thing
and settle for less of another. It is also possible, although far less easy, for us to alter the *aggregate
quantity and quality* of goods and services available to
be enjoyed during any period of time. The question of
how one organizes a society so as to obtain reasonable assurance that resources are deployed effectively, that is, deployed continuously and over time so
as to yield the maximum aggregate amounts of human
satisfactions, is of course the classic and central question to which the science of economics is addressed.

To assert that there is a pollution problem or an
environmental problem is to assert, at least implicitly,
that one or more resources is not being used so as to
maximize human satisfactions. In this respect at least
environmental problems are economics problems,
and better insight can be gained by application of
economic analysis. It would not be appropriate in this
context to attempt any comprehensive presentation of
the methodology of economic analysis, but I do want
to develop briefly four or five of the key premises of
that system of analysis, partly for the purposes of re-
freshing recollections of those readers who have some

familiarity with the analysis, and partly for the purpose of making clear to all the sense in which I will be using certain terms.

One can imagine a society in which each individual, or at least each family unit, attempts to provide for all its needs: builds its own shelter, raises its own crops, does its own hunting, fashions its own clothing, and so forth. There have been such societies, and some may still exist in remote portions of the globe. Obviously the inhabitants of such a society must live at a bare subsistence level, for there can be no automotive plows and reapers, no refrigeration units to preserve foods from harvest season to harvest season, and not even any steel from which to construct durable handtools. And in such a society there can be very little leisure; all we know of such societies instructs us that people in these circumstances spend the overwhelming preponderance of waking hours in attempts to improve their material situation, leaving almost no time either for recreation or enjoyment of music, art, or the other restorative activities to which leisure time may be put.

It is the phenomenon of specialization that makes less brutish forms of existence possible. The aggregate amount of all goods and services available to a society can be very substantially increased if those who are the most talented farmers spend all their time in farming, the best craftsmen spend all their time building shelters and tools, and if the Mozarts and Tolstoys are able to devote their time to the creation for themselves and others of repositories of pleasure and aesthetic insights. But if each individual's consumption pattern remains highly diversified, as it will, then the occurrence of highly specialized production patterns dictate that extensive patterns of exchange must occur.

A most important point that I wish to make about the phenomenon of exchange is that not just one but both parties to an exchange are better off after the exchange is executed than they were before.

Consider a typical instance of exchange. Mr. Farmer specializes in growing potatoes and Mr. Craft specializes in producing clothing. In their capacity as consumers, Mr. Farmer may be extremely fond of potatoes and Mr. Craft extremely fond of fine clothes. But in all probability Mr. Farmer will be better off if he has one suit of clothing than if he retains his tenth ton of potatoes, and Mr. Craft will probably be better off if he has a few pounds of potatoes rather than retaining the twenty-seventh suit he has manufactured this year. I say these trades are "probably" of advantage to the parties to stress that every adult, unless he has been found mentally incompetent, should be permitted to make his own judgment about what will advance his own well-being. And so, if these parties decide to exchange some quantity of potatoes for a suit of clothing, each by his own assessment will be better off as a consequence. Each has given up something which he wanted less, generally because he possessed it in comparative abundance to that for which he traded it, and each has obtained something that he wanted comparatively more. If each of these parties is benefited by the exchange and if no one else in the society is injured by it, then it necessarily follows that the aggregate level of satisfactions in the community as a whole has been increased by the exchange.

To this point I have written of our economy as if exchanges generally occurred by means of barter. This of course is not so, but it is a useful style of thought and expression to ignore the existence of money because people are far more apt to make serious analytical errors when they begin thinking and talking of goods being exchanged for money rather than for other goods. What money really is, and what its function is, can best be illustrated by reference again to a mytical and primitive society. In our primitive but now specialized barter society, a man's income is rigidly linked to his own production in two important senses. First what he is able to consume himself over a period of time is strictly limited by the value which people in the society attach to what he produces—that is to say, how much they are willing to exchange for what he produces. In short, income distribution is strictly determined by individual productivity.

But there is a second constraint, and that is that a man's productive activity will often have to be as incessant and continuous as he would like his consumption activity to be. He must have potatoes at hand when he wants a suit of clothing. Whether it is feasible to work very hard at producing potatoes for a while and then perhaps take a vacation depends entirely on the feasibility of storing potatoes. In such a society savings must occur in physical forms, and the potato farmer is somewhat better off in this respect than the egg farmer, whose product will not store well at all. The first occasion on which an egg farmer delivers substantial quantities of his production in the spring and obtains in exchange for it, not physical goods, but a promise from others that they will deliver goods to the egg farmer during his summer vacation then, for practical purposes, money has been introduced into the economy.

Money itself satisfies no human needs—it is merely a form of credit or an accounting system. It consists of claim checks, redeemable at subsequent points in time, against the productive activities of others. The aggregate flow of money per unit of time in a society is worth precisely as much as the aggregate production of goods and services in the economy in that period of time. If more units of money are produced, the value of each unit of money simply falls so as to maintain that equality. In short, the money stock of an economy is totally irrelevant to the wealth or well-being of the society in any sensible terms. The level of well-being is determined by the aggregate quantities of goods and services that are available to be enjoyed.

Let us change the situation slightly and assume that our egg farmer wants to go on winter vacation *before* he has gotten ahead by delivering his large crop of spring eggs. He is now in the position of saying to others, "Supply me with my needs while I am on vacation and after I return I will deliver eggs in exchange for what you provide." There will be some exchange rate for eggs and each of the other types of goods which he wants—let us say, one dozen eggs for one sack of potatoes—exchanged on a *current delivery* basis. But now the egg farmer is asking the potato farmer to defer his consumption of eggs for the period of the credit extended. Presumably the potato farmer is in a position to go on exchanging his potatoes with other egg farmers at the prevailing exchange rate. To induce the potato farmer to defer his consumption of eggs in order to make possible the egg farmer's vacation, it is certain that the egg farmer will have to offer a more favorable exchange rate. Let us just say that he is willing to deliver fifteen spring eggs for a sack of winter potatoes. This difference in value between eggs delivered presently and eggs to be delivered in the future is a reward to the potato farmer for the service of delaying the consumption that corresponds to one's productive activities. It is an interest rate.

In a society that functions at bare survival levels, the feasibility of delaying the consumption that corresponds to one's current productive activities is sharply limited; the supply of credit, or capital, will be small and interest rates will be relatively high. In a more affluent society there are a larger number of persons around who are in a position to consume less than all they are entitled to consume at any particular point in time, and interest rates characteristically will be relatively lower. Obviously there are other factors that affect the level of interest rates, and my suggested generalization that interest rates will be higher in less affluent societies is overbroad; but the point has a basic validity, and it focuses sharply on what interest rates really are. They are the rewards one receives for permitting someone else to consume presently what the lender is entitled to consume on the basis of his own productive activities. This service of deferring one's own consumption and transferring to others entitlement to present consumption is a very real service, and it is for this service that interest payments are made. The presence in the society of persons who are willing to provide that service is an important resource of the society.

Let me give an example of why this service is so vital. Suppose that up until some point in time there have been no plows in our primitive society—no one has ever thought of one, much less built one. But then Mr. Craft conceives of the idea of a plow and decides he will try to build one. He appreciates that it will be a long and uncertain project, taking all of his time for about six months. During that time, not only will he have to eat but he will have to acquire the lumber and metal from which a plow is to be made. If there were no possibility of separating the rate at which a man currently produced goods intended for the consumption of himself and others from the rate at which he himself consumed, then it would not be feasible for Mr. Craft to take his highly creative vacation and to confer upon his community the benefits of the plow. The entire process of investment—the development of tools or ideas which do not satisfy current consumption needs but rather give rise to the possibility of increased future rates of production of goods and services —necessarily involves the diversion of productive resources from current production for consumption purposes. This can only occur if someone in the society is willing to defer consumption—to save—to an extent coextensive with the magnitude of the investment. It is the saver's deferral of his own present consumption that allows resources to be channeled into the investment activity. One of the dilemmas that confronts a primitive society is that, because it functions at a bare subsistence level, the feasibility of deferring consumption and saving is very limited; and yet it is only by deferring consumption and saving that investment, which will increase productive capacities and the living standards of the community in the future, is made possible.

Finally, I wish to emphasize that there is no *inevitable* link between individual productive capacities and income distribution in a society. To make the point, let me introduce into our mythical society one additional individual, an unfortunate fellow born with a serious physical defect which makes it impossible for him to make any significant contribution to the aggregate well-being of the society. He has nothing to exchange, and therefore nothing to consume apart from the generosity of others. But the society may decide to share with him some fraction of their aggregate production, motivated by generosity and compassion or, in the alternative, motivated by a concern that this disadvantaged individual will prove to be not merely unproductive but actually destructive of the society if his deprivation is too great. Probably, although not necessarily, through a collective device called government, they may levy taxes upon themselves and transfer to the disadvantaged man some fractional share of their production. This may be done in the form of transfers of actual goods and services, which the recipient will then be in a position to exchange for still other goods and services so as to compose that particular combination of consumption goods which he individually prefers. Income transfers of this kind can be made much more efficiently of course if the society has a monetary system, for it is easier both to collect and to distribute claim checks than it is to distribute goods themselves.

There is no necessary incompatibility between redistributions of income of this sort on the one hand and, on the other, keeping all resources efficiently employed so that the aggregate output of the society is as high as possible. Indeed in the long run, the practical possibility of making income redistributions is facilitated by maintaining the efficient deployment of resources. Such deployment increases the aggregate well-being of the community as a whole, and income redistributions then impinge less painfully on the contributing members of the society.

The next concept I wish to note is that of cost and, in particular, the very important distinction between, on one hand, mere *income transfers,* which often are referred to as costs by persons on the losing end and, on the other, events or activities which diminish the aggregate stock of resources available to the community and thus are properly regarded as being *costs* to the community as an aggregate. For example, to return to the case of our disadvantaged individual to whom income transfers were made, we might say in a colloquial sense that each of the other members of the community incurred cost in the amount of taxes he paid to support those transfer payments. But it is clear that the wealth of the community as a whole is unaffected by such payments; the total stock of resources is no less after the transfer than before. In economic terms this type of wealth redistribution is described as a *private* cost to those who pay, and that type of event is carefully distinguished from a different phenomenon which is called a *social* cost. Any activity that uses up the resources of the society and thus precludes devotion of those resources to other uses represents a social cost. Thus the production of an automobile requires a certain amount of human energy, of iron ore, of coal and limestone to turn the iron ore into steel, of glass, and so forth. It is possible to express the social cost of an automobile in several ways: it can be described by listing the resources which were consumed in its production, or by stating the monetary value of the resources that were consumed in its production; or if it is the case that those same quantities of human energy, coal, limestone, and iron ore would have been sufficient to produce seven washing machines, two toasters, and one microscope, then the cost of the automobile can be expressed in terms of those alternative sources of satisfaction that were foregone as a consequence of its production.

Obviously an activity that yields sources of human satisfaction is not bad merely because it has social costs; all such activities have some social cost. In a well-arranged society every unit of resources is deployed in such a way that the ratio of human satisfactions yielded to a social cost incurred is as high as possible. If any resource can be shifted from a first deployment to a second, and it would yield a larger amount of human satisfaction in the second, then it should be so shifted.

Finally we should note that if individuals in a society are free to engage in whatever exchanges of resources are mutually satisfactory for themselves then, at least in theory, every resource in the society will be deployed in the way that yields the greatest possible human satisfaction. Let me give a simple example of how this comes about. Suppose Farmer No. 1 is devoting his time and arable land to the production of string beans which others in the society enjoy and therefore value at some rate of exchange for the things they themselves are producing. Assume further that others in the society would be willing to exchange more of what they produce for the amount of wheat that could be grown on the land than they are willing to exchange for string beans that can be grown. As soon as anyone else in the society perceives this circumstance, and let us assume that it is Farmer No. 2 who first perceives it, he is in a position to buy the land from Farmer No. 1 and devote the land to its more productive wheat-growing use. Farmer No. 1 will value his land in terms of the stream of goods which he is able to obtain for the string beans he grows on it. Farmer No. 2 will value the same land in terms of the larger stream of goods and services that he will be able to obtain in exchange for the wheat which he expects to be able to grow on it. Thus the land is more valuable to Farmer No. 2 than to Farmer No. 1, and he will be able to offer Farmer No. 1 a price higher than the minimum price Farmer No. 1 will demand to relinquish the land.

The disparity between these two evaluations may be substantial, and it is not possible to say at what precise value transfer will occur, but it will occur at some price not less than its value in string bean production and not more than its value in wheat production. Both will be better off after the transaction: Farmer No. 1 will have claim checks that will obtain for him more than he would have been able to obtain with his string beans; Farmer No. 2 will be able to obtain more goods and services in exchange for the wheat he grows than he would have been able to obtain for the claim checks he delivered to Farmer No. 1; and of course the society as a whole will be better off because it values the wheat more highly than the string beans.

This set of concepts constitutes the basic underpinnings of an efficiently organized society. Each individual should be located in that specialized occupation in which he can contribute most to the satisfaction of himself and of others in the society. And those who have the skills and foresight to employ resources so that those resources make the largest possible contribution are in a position to obtain those resources, and so employ them, from others who are employing them less effectively. Income redistributions to the disadvantaged are by no means precluded; neither are they inconsistent with the optimum deployment of all the resources.

The only question that remains is why things do not in fact seem to work out as well in our free-market economy as this neat set of premises suggests they should. Four types of difficulties can intrude upon this smoothly functioning system. Two of these are almost entirely irrelevant to our present concerns, and I will merely note them. The first, and the only one of the four that was clearly recognized and analyzed prior to the depression of the 1930s, is the problem of privately created monopolies such as price conspiracies and territorial divisions which require government intervention to terminate their harmful effects.

The second type consists of problems of macroeconomic balance involving such matters as government fiscal and monetary policy. It was our basic ignorance of these policies that led to the great depression of the 1930s and precluded any rapid solution. That episode extensively and unjustifiably undermined the confidence of our population in free-market mechanisms, which were not in fact responsible for the difficulties.

The third and fourth types of problems with which the government must concern itself if market systems are to work adequately are directly relevant to environmental problems and require fuller discussion. The third problem is that of income distribution and our societal unwillingness to face up to this problem honestly. The economic history of the United States for the last forty years is a catalog of instances in which we, acting through government, have confused problems of income distribution with problems of efficient use of resources. We observe a segment of the society whose income position we regard as unsatisfactory —let us say farmers. Then, rather than directly and openly improving their income position to the extent that we, as society, think appropriate by making income transfers to them, we attempt to improve their income positions by blocking free exchange—for example, by setting artificially high prices for wheat or cotton. This in turn leads to an inefficiently large devotion of resources—of land and human energy—to the production of those goods; and then further bureaucratic constraints on free exchange are necessary to avoid overproduction. Consequently we wind up with a very inadequate mechanism of income redistribution and at the same time one that is enormously wasteful of the resources of the country. Precisely the same point could be made with respect to the trucking industry, the airline industry, the petroleum industry, the maritime industry, and a host of other industries in which at some particular point in time, we as a society were unhappy with the income patterns we observed in those fields. This matter of income distribution does have a good deal to do with our current problems of pollution, but I want to put off for the moment explaining what that relationship is and turn instead to the fourth of the defects to be discussed, the relationship of which to environmental problems is somewhat more self-evident.

The fourth problem might be called any of a variety of names: that of imprecisely defined ownership or, alternatively, that of bad accounting by local decision-makers. The technical economic term for the concept is "externality." For the purposes of this text, I will use another phrase because it has been used elsewhere in environmental literature. I will refer to the problem as the "problem of the commons." Whatever name is used, the concept is important and requires full elaboration.

Only comparatively recently have economists and lawyers fully recognized the existence of a strong interaction between legal concepts of ownership or property and the smooth functioning of an economic system. Clearly defined and effectively enforced concepts of ownership have major impacts on individual incentives. For example, I have referred to Farmer No. 1 owning land on which he raised string beans. In that context the concept of ownership is reasonably precise: it is the exclusive right to use and exploit a particular resource. Thus Farmer No. 1 could address himself to the question whether he should build an irrigation system for his land or spread fertilizer upon it, all on the assumption that he would reap the benefits of those activities if he chose to engage in them. His incentives and his behavior would have been far different if he had been unable to prevent interlopers from coming in, using his lands, and reaping the benefits of those improvements after he had made them. Management of resources to which all, or even many, have equal or uncontrolled access is very difficult. In my opinion the great preponderance of our environmental problems are attributable to the fact that the resources critically involved are owned by, or at least available to, larger numbers of people in common.

To illustrate this point let me develop another very simple hypothetical case. Let us suppose that a man owns a large parcel of land—in the Sierra, perhaps —that is not accessible to anyone else, and has on it a small lake. Man No. 1, we will call him, likes to fish. There is an ample stock of trout in the lake, and there are no fish or game laws that apply to the situation. Nevertheless, Man No. 1 makes up some rules for himself in order to preserve the quality of fishing for his future years. He decides that at least on most days he will not take more than six or seven trout and, because he prefers catching large fish to small ones, he decides to put back any fish under eight inches. His reasoning is perfectly sound: what he does not take out of the lake this year he will be able to take out of the lake next year or the year after that. To put the matter somewhat differently, every fish he catches this year has a cost to him—it represents a fish that he will not be able to catch the following year. And since he has a strong interest in preserving the quality of fishing over the years, he behaves in the fashion I have described.

But now let us suppose the ownership situation changes and fifty other families build cabins on the lake and are entitled to fish there. Man No. 1's reasoning process changes: it is no longer true that a fish that he fails to take out of the lake at the present time represents one he will be able to take out at a subsequent point in time. Indeed, in view of the numbers involved, it is far more likely that any fish he does not catch today will be caught tomorrow or next week by one of the other fifty fishermen on the lake. In economic terms, the situation can be described in the following way. Originally, Man No. 1 paid an opportunity cost every time he took a fish from the lake: *his* fish population had been diminished; each time he took a fish he diminished the prospect of pleasure and excitement and nourishment that would have been available for him on a subsequent occasion. After the other fifty families appear, his taking a fish no longer has that cost *to him*, for there is no assurance he will be able to take that fish on a subsequent occasion—rather, the odds are to the contrary.

This very simple story is one of great importance in our economy and in our world, and represents a very pervasive phenomenon. Good conservation practices are implicit in carefully defined and enforced situations of ownership. With respect to a piece of property which a man owns in an enforceable sense and from which he can exclude others, he has very strong incentives to exploit it at a gradual and carefully considered rate that gives due attention to the future. This is so whether he is preserving the unused portion for his own subsequent enjoyment or is merely intending to preserve the value of his property so as to be able to transfer it at a high price in the future. Again, he is calculating a trade-off between present enjoyment and future enjoyment; and whether he thinks explicitly in these terms or not, he employs in that calculation something of a discount rate or interest rate by which he evaluates the comparative advantages of present as opposed to future enjoyment. But wherever we encounter a situation where ownership rights are imprecisely defined—where what a man owns is his only when and because he grabs it, and where the benefit belongs to someone else if someone else grabs it first—then all normal incentives for private conservation are destroyed and the resource will be exploited at an excessive and wasteful rate.

3

The Problem of the Commons
and Its Regulation

The problem of the commons is the primary source of our environmental and conservation difficulties. I want to develop that theme first with a particular historic example, and then with several current ones. The historic example has to do with the production of natural gas and petroleum. In the late 1920s and early 1930s there was widespread outcry about conservation practices in the petroleum industry—production rates were inordinately high and prices very depressed. These conditions then were

widely thought to be just another aspect of the depression and that view still prevails in some quarters.
However, I think these phenomena were largely independent of the depression, and I will offer you another
view of them.

Natural Resources

Oil and gas are produced from underground pools
subject to natural pressure that will drive the oil or gas
up through the well once it has been drilled. If an
individual or single company owned all the land overlying a petroleum pool, he would make certain calculations (rather like those of our single fisherman) about
the rate at which he would produce from that pool.
Basically, he would want to produce in a way that
generated the largest possible difference between his
costs and his revenues. How much oil should he take
from the pool this year, how much next year, and so on,
to attain this profit-maximizing goal? If too much oil is
produced in the current year, the price will fall—
eventually it will fall below the out-of-pocket costs of
pumping it and getting it to market. Clearly production
will be halted then. But there is a factor in addition to
current market price and production costs that the
owner will take into account. He would be foolish to
produce and sell a barrel of oil this year for a dollar if he
could sell that barrel next year for a substantially
higher price—say, two dollars. Of course he would

rather have a dollar of income this year than just a dollar of income next year; but depending on the level of prevailing interest rates, he would be indifferent between a dollar of income this year and perhaps $1.06 of income in the second year, and perhaps $1.13 of income in the third year, assuming a 6 percent interest rate. Thus he would leave oil in the ground whenever its future expected value exceeded present value by more than the interest rate.

In sum, such a unified producer would conserve his pool over time because he would recognize that there were two elements of cost to him of removing from the pool currently any given barrel of oil: 1) his out-of-pocket production cost; 2) a cost attributable to the foregone opportunity of selling that barrel at a subsequent point in time; and he would slow the rate of present exploitation so that the sum of these costs did not exceed prevailing price. Since the subsequent price will be higher than the present price in most extractive industries because of the expanding demands of the society for the minerals and because of the gradual depletion of our aggregate stock of minerals and the resultant scarcity, this consideration markedly reduces extraction rates. Since higher future market prices are discounted to present value by a compounded interest rate, current production occurs at a socially desirable rate if unified ownership exists.

However, at the time under consideration, it was not generally the case that a single individual or firm owned all of the surface rights that overlay the petroleum pool. It was far more common for a very large number of owners to have parcels overlying the pool. And the property laws of many of the states that were important petroleum producers at that time were not conducive to desirable rates of production. In effect the laws said that a man owned a barrel of petroleum when it came out of the ground through his well. Consequently, it was not sensible for any individual producer to think in terms of the foregone opportunity to produce a barrel of oil next year if he did not produce it this year. If he did not produce it this year, someone else was likely to pull it out through that person's well. And the consequence was a race among the competing producers overlying the field, each to produce as rapidly as possible and get as much as he could out through his well before others took it out through theirs.

The type of property rule involved in this situation is often referred to as a *rule of capture*, for obvious reasons. And as we shall see, a variant of the rule of capture continues to prevail in a large number of contexts. I think it is possible to make the general assertion that wherever a large number of independent persons or business entities, operating under a rule of capture, share in common access to a supply or inventory of an exhaustible resource, they will consume and exhaust that resource at an inappropriately rapid rate.

This particular aspect of the problem of the commons comes up in a variety of contexts, some profound and some mundane. Let me offer a trivial but, I think, amusing example. I have a perceptive colleague who takes some pleasure in finding earthy applications of important principles. I once heard him express the principle to which I have been referring in a form I now call "Barnett's Lunch Law." Barnett's Lunch Law goes as follows: If six or more people go to lunch, the bill is always divided evenly rather than apportioned on the basis of what each person actually ordered. Therefore if six or more people go to lunch, each, to assure that he is not cheated, will order the most expensive thing on the menu. As an aside I suggest to you that Barnett's Lunch Law has important application to the behavior of our state and federal legislatures, but elaboration of that application must await a differently titled publication.

Manufactured Goods

The preceding examples have shown that unduly high consumption rates are caused by common access to a stock of some natural resource. A different manifestation of the same basic problem appears where there is common access to a supply of goods which is not supplied by nature but must be brought into existence by private activity. In such circumstances, because the problem of the commons will operate after the supply is created, no one has adequate incentives to create the supply in the first place. Society's aggregate supply of knowledge or inventions is an example.

Compare the incentives confronting a man who has a choice between investing in a shoe factory and investing in research by which he hopes to discover a better mousetrap. If he invests in a shoe factory, there is no ambiguity about his ownership of the shoe factory, the shoes produced in it, and the proceeds that can be obtained by selling the shoes. He will invest $100 in a shoe factory if he expects that it will produce a stream of shoes that can be exchanged or sold for a stream of receipts that has a present value of more than $100. And that is also the socially optimum level of investment in shoe factories.

But if he considers investing $100 in discovering a better mousetrap, then in the absence of any special legal institution that will assist him, it is not at all clear that he will be able to produce mousetraps and exchange them for receipts, or other goods and services, that are commensurate with the value that other persons attach to having the better mousetrap that he has developed. The reason for this is that knowledge —knowledge in this case of how to build a better mousetrap—almost inevitably turns out to be something to which we all have common access. It will be difficult both to sell the new mousetrap and to keep his development secret; yet as soon as the secret is lost, others may copy his development and sell mousetraps in competition with him. Unlike him, however, the copiers will not have made the initial investment in development; competition will force prices down to the point where they are just adequate to cover his and his competitors' production costs. In all probability he will be unable to recover his development costs. This, of course, is precisely the problem to which our patent laws are addressed. There is every reason to expect, in a competitive economy, that the flow of investment into research and development would be far less than socially optimum unless we either had a patent system or, in the alternative, provided government subsidies for research and development.

This second aspect of the problem of commonality might be stated as follows: Where the fruits of investment will be commonly available for the benefit of all, then individual incentives to make such investments will be inadequate and the aggregate devotion of resources in the society to that form of investment will be less than optimum.

I do not mean to suggest that these two different aspects of the problem of the commons are profoundly different. They are opposite sides of the same coin, and in some contexts it is difficult to decide which is the more appropriate to describe the phenomenon that one is observing. Consider the use of the water in a lake, for example. There are many persons along its shores, each of whom is free to withdraw water for a variety of purposes. None has very strong incentives to conserve water, to use it sparingly. What one does not withdraw today someone may withdraw tomorrow. Neither does anyone have adequate incentives to invest in purification devices which would restore the water to its original clean state before it runs back into the lake by seepage or otherwise. Such an investment would be an investment in producing a clean lake, and a clean lake will be equally accessible to all so that the investor will experience private gains that are far less than the aggregate of the benefits that he has conferred upon the community as a whole by his investment in purification devices.

Let me try to state explicitly the point I have been driving at with this series of illustrations. Our environmental problems have many aspects. There are difficult scientific questions about what is harmful when it is dumped into our air or into our water. There are difficult medical and genetic questions involved in assessing the extent of harm caused by these agents even after they have been identified as harmful to some degree. There are enormously difficult engineering questions to be faced in altering the industrial or other processes by which those ingredients now are introduced in excessive amounts. But even after all these questions have been answered with as much certainty as will ever be possible, there remains the very difficult problem of creating adequate incentives on the part of individuals and companies to take full advantage of the knowledge that has been provided by the fields of science and engineering. This is so because invariably there will be substantial private costs that must be incurred in order to yield the benefits we desire, and yet the benefits will accrue to a very large number of very widely diversified individuals so that it will not be feasible to recover from each beneficiary a price that corresponds to the satisfaction conferred upon him. Therefore the person who engages in providing social benefits of this sort generally finds it impossible to gather for himself a revenue stream, to gather private benefits, adequate to compensate him for the private costs that he has incurred. The activity will take place to an insufficient extent.

Land Preservation

Let me take a series of contemporary environmental problems and offer more concrete illustrations of how these principles work out in practice. For a starter, take a problem that has no serious technological aspects: the question of preserving undeveloped some optimum amount of timber and grasslands in the foothills of the San Francisco peninsula. The case for having some quantity of such lands is very strong. All who live in the area derive aesthetic enjoyment from walking through them, even looking at them from our patios or as we drive past them on the highways. Such lands serve as sanctuaries for wildlife, which we enjoy in similar ways; and they help to preserve the equable climate of the area we all enjoy. But of course someone owns those lands and there are alternative uses to which they can be put. Let us assume that the alternative uses are less valuable to the community as a whole than is their retention in a wholly undeveloped state.

The difficulty is that the private owners have practicable ways of obtaining a stream of private receipts from the lands when they are put into alternative uses, such as housing or industrial development, or even farming, or harvesting the timber that stands on the lands. But the owner has no practicable way of selling to each of us, i.e., exchanging for the goods and services that each of us produces, the benefits that would be conferred upon us if the lands were kept in the natural state—benefits we would happily pay for rather than forego. If there were some practicable way of billing each of us for the amount we would be willing to pay for those benefits, then our traditional market systems would make it privately profitable to retain the lands in the natural state precisely because, by our assumption, that is the use that creates the largest stream of benefits. But because of the enormous number of people involved, and because of the impossibility of denying benefits to those who do not pay, that possibility is purely theoretical.

In a situation such as this, collective action, generally through local government, is the only realistic alternative. No *precise* determination will ever be possible either of the amounts of lands, or which particular lands, should remain undeveloped. In principle development should be allowed to proceed until development of one more parcel would yield a stream of marketable benefits of lesser magnitude than the stream of unmarketable benefits that would be provided by keeping that next parcel undeveloped. When this point has been reached, development should be halted by governmental action since the interaction of market systems will not bring it to a halt. When that point has been reached must be determined by political means, and I say that with full recognition that such political determinations generally will yield far less accurate results than would private market exchanges if, contrary to fact, such exchanges represented a practicable possibility.

But these observations leave open some of the most important questions. How is development to be stopped? We must recognize that forbidding the development of land held by a private individual has the consequence of effecting an income transfer from him to all of the other members of the community who will enjoy the benefits of nondevelopment. Indeed, this is true even if we do not ordain complete nondevelopment but merely restrict the use to which he may put the land by zoning it. The situation is no different than if we took the land physically from him, perhaps to build a school, which would similarly confer benefits on the community as a whole as opposed to the prior landowner. We are accustomed to the notion that the community must condemn land, it must pay for the diminution of value it imposes on the prior owners, when it physically takes land for such purposes as school construction. Any other course is prohibited by one of the most fundamental and ancient of constitutional prohibitions: that property shall not be taken for public use without just compensation. The most obvious justification for that constitutional principle is to guard against the unfairness of substantial and selective income redistributions from particular individuals to members of the community as a whole.

But there is a second and in some ways even more important objective that underlies that constitutional provision: the basic justification for taking the land at all is that it is more valuable to the community (including the owner) in the new public use than it is to the community in the privately profitable use to which the owner would put it. If this justification is truly available with respect to a given parcel, then it follows that the community can afford to pay the owner the market value of the land. For by assumption, the aggregate benefits that the community has received are greater in amount than are the marketable benefits which he could have produced by the alternative use, and those marketable benefits determine the market value of the land. The requirement of compensation therefore imposes a test on the good faith of members of the community: do they really believe that the value of the land, when put to the public use, is greater than its private value? If they do, they gain by condemning it, even though they must pay. If they do not, they should not condemn it. Apart from the requirement of compensation, there is no limit on the extent to which a selfish majority in the community may appropriate for their own benefits the invested savings of fortuitously selected individuals.

There is still another reason why a community

should proceed by way of condemnation. In any community not all lands will be developed simultaneously: first one parcel, then another is built upon, generally in the order in which the lands are best suited for development. When the point is reached at which development should stop, it makes eminently good sense that the parcels which happen to remain undeveloped be those selected to remain undeveloped indefinitely. Consider now a community in which the stopping point has not yet been reached. Consider the effect on incentives regarding development if all landholders in the community know that the rules of the game are to be that lands remaining undeveloped when the stopping point is reached will be taken without compensation. A very strong incentive for artificial development is created, an incentive to put the land to *some* commercial use, to assure that that parcel is not one of those whose private value is destroyed for the greater community good.

If the foothills are to be kept green, it is for the benefit of all of us who live here, and it is no more reasonable of us to expect to obtain those benefits without paying for the resources that confer them than it is for us to steal our food and clothing from the shelves of the local merchants.

Let me make one further observation—on the politics and income distribution effects of preserving undeveloped open spaces. The satisfactions that such lands provide are primarily aesthetic, and hence they must be seen as a kind of luxury good. If they are not in the same category as eight-year-old Scotch and European vacations, then certainly they fall near that end of the spectrum as opposed to basic food stuffs, clothing, and shelter. As is true of other luxury goods, the affluent, for perfectly sensible reasons, are prepared to devote not only more money but a much larger proportion of their disposable income to such goods, than are the poor. The decision to provide these satisfactions must be made politically—on something like a one-man, one-vote basis. Some quantity will be provided by government; that particular quantity will be available to all, and it will represent to each of us some particular fraction of his total of satisfactions. In terms of its social cost, although not in terms of the subjective satisfaction it yields, that quantity of environmental amenity will represent a much larger fraction of the total consumption of the poor than of the rich—precisely the opposite of the ratio which those income groups would choose to buy if the amenity was available on a free market. This much is inevitable; it is quite typical of political decisions with respect to resource use, that they are not susceptible to the degree of individuation that market decisions afford. The great advantage of free markets, which unfortunately will not work in this context, is that they afford each man the freedom to make his own choices on the basis of his own tastes. Not only the decision to provide *some* such satisfactions through undeveloped lands, but also the decision whether to provide somewhat more or somewhat less will be made politically; and the potential for conflict between different income groups is obvious. The rich will be disposed toward more of this luxury good and the poor toward less. Indeed, this conflict is already quite apparent in our political dialogues. Hardly a day passes that some black action group does not label the pursuit of environmental amenities a political cop-out designed to distract attention from their much more fundamental needs.

These facts have obvious implications for the kind of tax system by which the public acquisition of these amenities should be financed: it should be a distinctly progressive tax system, not only because payments will then be more nearly commensurate with benefits derived, but because such financing will diminish inter–income-group conflict and will diminish political resistance to the provision of such amenities and in the long run will enable us to have a larger, perhaps approximately optimum, amount of them.

Airport Noise

For the sake of noting some contrasts, let me shift from the comparatively simple problem of retaining undeveloped lands to the much more complex problem of airplane landing and take-off noise in airport vicinities. The variables are numerous: how far from the central cities should airports be built? Remote locations expose fewer people to airplane noise but entail far greater surface transport costs to and from the airport and expose more people to highway noise. What are the comparative advantages to spending money—that is, consuming resources—in making the airplane itself quieter as opposed to installing sound-proofing in the buildings in the airport vicinity? Would it be wise to prohibit by law residential construction within a large area around airports? To condemn and tear down residences located there when the airport was built? To contemplate the matter further, note that the sensible answers will vary markedly from airport to airport. From the standpoint of O'Hare Airport in Chicago, a substantial investment in making airplanes quieter could be justified; but such investments would be absurd from the standpoint of the airport in Las Vegas. Yet the same airplane that takes off from O'Hare will land in Las Vegas. These questions are far too complex to be answered with even a semblance of accuracy by any panel of experts, and to make matters worse, even if we knew the correct answers for today, they would prove to be incorrect answers for tomorrow. For the correct answers will change over time as the several technologies change: the technology of noise-suppression on airplanes, the technology of sound-proofing, the technology of local transit systems.

When questions are as complex as these are, and when they have the dynamic quality these questions do, then in my opinion it is a monstrous error, if any alternative is available, to commit them to government for *decision about what physical measures* should be adopted. In this context, government means federal government, and solutions to difficult problems rendered by the federal government have certain characteristics: the questions are threshed out once with vigorous, even bitter, controversy; then a single national compromise is adopted; and that national resolution, once adopted, is inordinately difficult to change for many, many years thereafter. Our most important single criterion regarding the solution to the problem of airport noise must be to assure that we preserve private incentives to advance each of the several technologies described previously. And that requires that different physical solutions be open to different airports and to different airlines at different points of time. It is a problem that should be left to the dynamic interaction of free markets if we can possibly find a way to make those markets work, and the proper question for government decision is how to repair those markets.

The reason the market in noise is not working now is, again, the problem of the commons. The resource involved is quietness—the absence of unpleasant noise. The resource of quiet exists in abundant but limited quantities, and it can either be consumed as an amenity in conjunction with residential living and other human activity, or in the alternative, it can be consumed in greater or lesser degrees by aviation transport and other forms of inherently noisy activity. Airplanes can never be made silent; if we are to have some air transport, as surely we must and will, then some of our quietness resource will be consumed by that activity. The important question is how much air transport and how noisy.

We have no precise ownership rules with respect to the resource of quiet. It is accessible to each of us as an individual and to the airlines, all without cost. Since there is no pricing mechanism which informs us of the value that resource has as an amenity, it is to be expected that quiet will be consumed not sparingly but voraciously by noisy activities. If by consuming 99 cents worth of engineering talent and other resources, the aircraft industry can avoid using a dollar's worth of aluminum, it will do so because it is profitable to do so. Even if the commitment of those same resources would avoid consuming a dollar's worth of quiet, the aircraft industry has no incentive to do so because according to today's rules, although it must pay for aluminum, it need not pay for quiet.

I do not mean to suggest that the executives who run the aircraft industries are bad men any more than I meant to suggest that the petroleum executives who produced at excessive rates when confronted by the rule of capture were bad men. There is a defect in our market mechanisms and executives are responding sensibly, just as you or I would in a competitive regime. In this context I am convinced that the right solution is neither to damn the industry nor to ask government to ordain a technology-stagnating answer to the question of how noisy airplanes should be permitted to be, but to change our property rules just as we changed the rule of capture regarding oil in the 1930s, so that a private market in the resource of quietness will function and will restore private incentives to use that resource sparingly. I am convinced that, whenever it is practicable to bring new free markets into existence by attributing property rights to a resource, that will prove to be the wisest course in the long run. That approach will not work in many environmental contexts, but the problem of noise in airport vicinities is one that can be attacked in that way.

Basically, the reason it is possible to approach the airport noise problem by fashioning markets in quietness is because the effects are localized. If one measures noise in an airport vicinity on a scale that takes into account both the intensity of noise exposure and the frequency with which any given point is exposed to noise of varying intensities, it is possible to draw a series of contour lines around the airport—that is, lines which join all the points on the ground that are exposed to similar quantities of noise as measured on that scale. The resulting map looks rather like a topographical map that shows the elevation of hills and valleys. The areas exposed to intense noise levels may stretch out considerable distances along the axes of the principal runways, but in other directions the noise contours will cut back reasonably close to the airport itself. Therefore, some of the lands and buildings in the community, usually including residential structures, will be exposed to intense airport noise and some will not. Both near the airport and relatively far from it, lands and buildings that are roughly comparable in all respects except for that of noise will be bought and sold. People in the community have a choice, whether to live in the noisy areas or to live in the quiet ones. For simplicity's sake I will use the term residences, since those are the properties most dramatically affected, but the principle is the same as to any type of building or as to undeveloped parcels of land. Obviously people would prefer to live in quiet residences than in noisy ones, and therefore the market value of comparable residences in the noise-exposed areas will be depressed. But the residence in the noisy areas will not fall to a market value of zero; some families will take advantage of the opportunity to obtain at a low price a larger and better residence than they could otherwise afford, and they will exercise their choice for more house and less quiet. The difference in value between comparable residences which are and are not exposed to aircraft noise serves as an accurate measure of the cost of noise, or value of quietness, at the location of the lower-cost house. Of course the two properties will never be precisely the same in all other relevant respects, so I do not mean to exaggerate the precision with which this evaluation process can be made, but nevertheless it will afford a reasonably accurate measure.

In substance, my suggestion is that an airport be required to compensate surrounding landowners for the amount their property values were depressed by the presence of aircraft noise. The airports in turn would raise their landing fees and pass these costs on to the airlines. Higher landing fees would be charged to airlines operating noisy planes than to lines operating quieter ones. The use of the quieter planes would then be comparatively attractive to the airlines and they would be willing to pay more to an aircraft manufacturer that offered a quieter plane than to a manufacturer selling a noisier plane. The aircraft manufacturers in turn would thus be provided with economic incentives to advance the technology of noise-suppression and would build quieter planes. Indeed, it would be true that at every point along this vertical chain of relationships, the airport, the airlines, the airframe manufacturers, and the engine manufacturers: each would have an incentive to spend 99 cents in noise-suppressing measures if it would succeed in avoiding the necessity of paying one dollar in depressed property values to surrounding landholders. This is precisely the right set of incentives and would result in the right levels of expenditure on presently existing noise-suppressing devices and on research intended to improve the technology.

On the basis of this description, the system may not sound dramatically different from the system of noise easements that we have today. But there are two important differences. Under our present law in most parts of the country, the airport is not required to obtain a noise easement unless airplanes physically pass directly over the parcel of property involved.

Under this absurd rule, which is a technical hangover from ancient concepts of trespass, adjacent properties each affected in precisely the same way by exposure to noise are treated very differently. The one that happens to be directly under the flight path is compensated because a noise easement must be obtained; the adjoining parcel not under the flight path receives no compensation at all. That rule should be eliminated.

But a second major defect in our present system of noise easements is that the easement is perpetual. Once an easement has been acquired, the airline industry is entitled to go on making the same amount of noise forever without making any further payments. This makes a certain amount of sense, because the airline is required to pay, in the very first easement proceeding, the entire amount by which the value of the noise-exposed ownership interest has been depressed by noise exposure. The great difficulty caused by this feature of the system is that once the aviation industry has acquired a pattern of easements, no cost attaches to making noise in the future. Suppose that a major technological breakthrough should suddenly become available which made it possible, by spending several million dollars on each airplane perhaps, greatly to quiet the noise levels in airport vicinities. If the device were installed, property values in airport vicinities, because of the reduced noise levels, might increase in the aggregate by a sum vastly in excess of the costs of adopting the new technology. The social implications of the fact that land values did increase by a sum in excess of installation costs is that the devices should be installed. But the airlines would have no incentive to install them, because they would already have bought the right to go on making the old higher noise levels forever. They would not benefit from the rise in property values.

Therefore, in a long report I made to the FAA several years ago, I suggested another modification. Rather than paying the amount by which the permanent ownership value was diminished by noise and acquiring in exchange a permanent right to make noise, the airport would be required to make periodic payments to neighboring landowners in the amount by which the rental value, as opposed to the fair market value of the ownership interest, had been diminished during the preceding period. How long the periods are is not very critical. They might be two, or five, or ten years. What is important is that payment be made only for harm that has been done in the past, rather than for harm that is expected to occur in the future under the tacit assumption that noise levels will remain at their present intensity. This system, which I called a system of time-limited noise-easements, would preserve incentives on the part of the industry to strive for lower noise levels in the future. In the intervening years I have argued about the system with a variety of critics, and I have become ever more deeply convinced that the results of this system would be far superior to the results that one can reasonably expect from any system of certification administered by the FAA or, indeed, any other governmental entity. I think I can honestly say that the critics with whom I have argued have also become convinced, with the exception of those critics who are associated with the aviation industry or with the FAA.

The two examples I have discussed—preservation of undeveloped lands and airport noise—were selected because they are very different in two respects. With regard to the complexity of the physical solutions, the land problem is both simple and technologically static; the airport problem exceedingly difficult and technologically dynamic. From another vantage point, they differ in that I see no feasible way of solving the land problem by means of government action designed to make free markets work to solve the problem: direct government action appears to be necessary. The airport problem, on the other hand, can best be solved not by government ownership or specification of physical steps to be taken but by government repair of presently dysfunctional markets.

Almost all environmental problems require *some* kind of government action. But there are many different types of government intervention ranging from government ownership to legislature repair of free markets, and different types are appropriate to different problems. In the next chapter, I will canvass a wider variety of types of controls and attempt to suggest the types of problems to which each is best suited.

4

Modes of Legal
and Social Control

Let me start this chapter by asking you to focus on the features that are common to almost all environmental difficulties. A larger number of people or firms or municipalities are engaged in some generally useful activity. Mr. Smith is starting off to do an honest day's work in his brand new Brontosaurus 8, but he is pouring toxic substances from his tailpipe into our commonly shared reservoir of air. Company A is manufacturing paper products, but is discharging a variety of chemicals into our commonly shared river system.

These are not activites we desire to bring to a halt. In each case our objective is that the activity be modified in one or more ways. In some instances we would actually be better off with a much lesser quantity of the activity, but in the main the only realistic objective is to change the way the activity is carried on. More often than not, that means altering the technology of the activity. In bookkeeping terms, the new way of conducting the activity will be more "expensive" than the old; otherwise the persons involved would already have adopted the new technology out of their own self-interest, or would do so, as soon as the new technology became available, in the future. But in a more important sense the new method will actually be less costly—less preemptive of real scarce resources—than is the present method. The present method is cheaper only in the narrow sense that no payments need be made for some resource being used because ownership is legally defective; clearly that does not mean the resource is valueless. The behavioral mandate that we wish to issue is this: Spend another 99 cents on labor and machinery and land if those expenditures will enable you to avoid consuming, by soiling, clean air or clean water which we value at a dollar in alternative forms of satisfaction. Thus our objectives, soundly pursued, will make us all better off.

Government Don'ts

The problem is to find some technique which will induce the desired alteration in behavior. Consider the arsenal of governmental techniques employed down through history to induce behavioral changes. The most traditional of all is the criminal sanction. The criminal sanction will be of very limited utility here. It works well only when we are prepared to give negative orders in very specific terms and when the conduct prohibited is immediately and obviously harmful to some other individual. Don't rob banks. If that prohibition is disobeyed, we can safely assume that some banker will let us know about it. In the environmental context the criminal sanction scores badly on both counts. Simple, specific, and negative orders will not lead to sophisticated modification of production processes, and departures from the desired behavioral patterns, although they may be lethal to many over the years, do not yield visible and dramatic injuries which produce citizen complaints.

Criminal sanctions may prove useful in collateral ways. If we want companies to file reports on their activities, we might sensibly make the failure to file a report a crime and also make the filing of a false report a crime. To expect more of the criminal law is to court disappointment. Our experience in the food and drug field should convince us that only specific negative orders can effectively be enforced this way. And our experience with pornography, gambling, prostitution, and similar areas should convince us that the criminal law is effective only when there are complaining victims.

The second traditional government technique is to issue an order, perhaps a fairly complex one, to just one or to a small number of firms or individuals, to observe closely whether the order is obeyed, and then to impose punishment if it is not. Court injunctions, administrative cease-and-desist orders, and a variety of other governmental commands are of this type. Because the number of addressees is small, we can tailor the order to their situations so as to eliminate ambiguity, and we can watch closely to see whether they comply. For these reasons more complex orders, and indeed affirmative orders, can be enforced by this technique even though such orders cannot be handled well by the criminal process.

There are two reasons why this technique does not generally work well in the environmental context. First, the appropriate number of addressees often is unmanageably large. But, a more important second reason is this: Before someone can issue one of these highly complex orders he must have a large amount of information in order to know what command to issue. Despite these shortcomings, the governmental technique of tailormade commands is the technique on which we have primarily relied up to to this date.

The Tailormade Command Approach

For an illustration of reliance on that technique and for some insight into the difficulties that result, let us review the federal water pollution legislation of the last eighteen years. The basic act was passed in 1948 and was amended in 1956, 1961, 1965, 1966, and 1970. I will not trace sequentially through all the convolutions these amendments represented, but will merely describe the residual piece of legislation that is their product. The statute starts off by asserting that the individual states have both primary responsibility and primary control of water pollution. It provides for federal planning and for federal financial aid to the states and cities. It creates an advisory board to assist with the problem of gathering information. But the teeth of the legislation, insofar as it has any, lie in its provision for abatement orders—the issuance of tailormade commands by the Secretary of the Interior.

These orders can be issued only under very limited circumstances. Prior to 1961, a very limited category of lakes and rivers were covered, but now the act applies to virtually all the waters in the United States. Before any action can be taken it must be possible to show that harm is being caused. If the person or property harmed is in the same state as the pollution source, then the governor of that state can veto federal action. If the harm is caused to some other state, the Secretary must obtain the consent of one governor or the other, but neither one alone can veto federal action. The first procedural step is to send to the polluter a complaint about his conduct and a set of recommendations for cleaning it up. The Secretary must then wait a reasonable time to see whether the recommendations are accepted. If they are not, the Secretary may move to the second step.

The second step is to call a conference of the pollution agencies of all the affected states. This conference works out another set of recommendations to be sent to the polluter, which may or may not be the same as the Secretary's original recommendations. Again, a reasonable time must pass to see whether the recommendations are complied with. If they are not, step three becomes possible.

Step three is to appoint a hearing board. The statute specifies the composition of the board. There must be representatives from each state and from the Department of Commerce, as well as others. The board holds hearings and then frames still another set of recommendations, perhaps the same as the last, and again the passage of a reasonable time is required to see whether compliance occurs.

If the polluter still does not comply, the Secretary may take the fourth step, which is to commence suit against the polluter in a federal court. But the judge is specifically authorized by the statute to frame his own recommendations in this proceeding, and he is directed by the statute to take into account the practicality and the economic feasibility of any steps that he may order. If the polluter fails to comply with the court order, he may then be brought back to the federal court where, after a hearing, he will be held in contempt and either fined or sent to jail.

Notice that there is no possibility whatsoever that the polluter may ever suffer any punishment for failing to comply with any of the recommendations except those embodied in the order finally issued by the judge. If the recommended action will have private costs to him, as is almost invariably the case, he has every incentive to wait out all of these procedural complexities and take action only when ultimately confronted by the order from the court.

The statue is so replete with provisions for hearings and investigations that the temptation to poke fun at it is strong. Critics also are inclined to suggest that the multitudinous opportunities for delay were inserted by a cynical Congress at the behest of the "vested interests." The cynicism may not be wholly without basis, but I feel confident that, at least in part, the Congress was responding to a much more genuine difficulty. A sensible order cannot be issued until one has gathered an enormous amount and variety of information. Is there some purification process through which the effluent can be put? Would the addition of still other chemicals serve to neutralize its harmful effects? Is it possible that basic changes might be made in the technology of the offending plant so that the harmful effluent would not be produced at all? How much expense will be involved in any one of these approaches and to what extent will offsetting benefits be yielded by it?

The statute quite properly contemplates that all these questions will be asked and answered. One of the ironies about the statute is that much of the information which the enforcement officials are required to obtain is peculiarly within the knowledge of the polluter, but the polluter has no incentive to deliver it. Of course, there are subpoenas and other coercive techniques by which he can be compelled to disgorge the information, at least that which he has readily at hand. It is even more difficult to coerce someone to make studies, to learn new information which he readily could but has no particular incentive to learn.

But, let us assume that at long last, probably at considerable expense both to the polluter and to the government, the appropriate information is assembled by the polluter's employees and transmitted to the government's employees, who must then study it and assimilate it as best they can. Eventually an order is issued. Let us assume that it is the best and wisest order that could possibly have been issued, and that the polluter complies with it in every detail. Within a month, within a year, in all probability before the Secretary has finished his job with respect to the next plant on down the river, the state of the art at the first plant will have changed. There will be available some new device or process which would enable still lower levels of pollution to be obtained at the first plant. But the first polluter has no incentive whatsoever to adopt them. He is now in compliance with the order issued against him—he is doing everything the government has asked or expected him to do.

I submit as an obvious and unavoidable truth the proposition that if the first polluter had had the incentive to do so, he could have taken, of his own volition, and with vastly less administrative expense, action at least as wise as any likely to be ordered by the Secretary after elaborate investigation and enforcement proceedings. If he had the incentive to do so, he would adopt progressively each new advance in the technology available to him. If there is any technique of government available which would create such incentives, it seems plain to me that we should resort to it in preference to the technique of tailormade orders requiring specific physical solutions to be adopted.

The tailormade command approach is deficient in still another respect. The procedural complexities of the approach are such that the enforcement officials must, in almost all cases, focus their attention on one particular polluter or certainly a very small number. On any major river system there will be a large number of pollution sources. There is no particular reason to expect that the firm or handful of firms on which the Secretary first focuses his attention will be the one for which it is least costly to make major improvements. Large firms that contribute absolutely large quantities of effluents are probably first targets, both for political reasons and because one might guess, without further information, that they could make major improvements. But it may prove to be the case that a dozen smaller firms, by some much easier modification of their production processes, could yield a much more substantial gain.

But even this description of the problem makes it sound too simple. The real difficulty is that the river and all its polluters—industrial, municipal, agricultural—must be viewed as a single, interdependent system. It is not possible to say how much extra labor and steel Firm A should consume in order to achieve less pollution until that question has been answered for Firms B, C, D, and so forth. But the question cannot be answered for B or C until it has been answered for A, and so on around the circle. The desirable result can emerge only from a series of iterative steps in which each firm adjusts, and then later adjusts again, to what all other firms are doing at the time of each individual adjustment. Such an iterative approach toward a system equilibrium is unlikely to be achieved by issuance of government orders which must be preceded by elaborate investigatory procedures. It can only be achieved if the individual decision-making units have the freedom to act unilaterally and the incentive to act so as to minimize the aggregate resource costs (including clean water as a resource) of their operations. In other words, to succeed we must make the optimum level of pollution the most profitable level for the individual firm. As a practical matter, tailormade orders will not do the job.

Class Action and Effluent Tax

There are two techniques of government influence on behavior that we have not used extensively in this context and which I think would work far better than the regulatory techniques to which we have become wedded over the years. Those techniques are the class action and the effluent tax. Consider briefly how each of those devices might be applied to the water pollution problem we have been discussing. Those remedies can be advantageous with respect to environmental problems because they can substantially reduce the administrative costs and the information gathering costs that are prerequisite to making the correct decision about what should be done.

Let me emphasize that if the right decision is to be made, precisely the same information must be gathered no matter what governmental technique is used, that is, no matter who makes the decision. Regardless of the governmental technique used, someone must assemble relatively accurate information: first, with respect to the costs being imposed on the society by the pollutants in question; second, with respect to the technology being employed by the polluter and about alternative possible technologies which he might employ; and third, about the costs—both the traditional accounting costs and the social cost of residual pollution—of each technological alternative. The person who is going to make the decision about what physical steps should be taken must have this information if he is to make the decision at all wisely. The basic objective, as I have indicated before, is to adopt pollution-reducing measures which, in a bookkeeping sense, will be more expensive than the present technology, so long as each additional dollar spent on these measures yields at a dollar in benefits from pollution-reduction. Moreover, if the technology is a complex and changing one, as will often be the case, then it is necessary to gather this information and make the calculations not just once but again and again, as time passes.

The tailormade order approach implicitly assumes that some government official will be able to gather all this information. In the water pollution legislation, this assumption manifests itself in the various provisions for conferences and hearing boards. These cumbersome and expensive investigatory techniques are used by the official to extract, from a reluctant and perhaps recalcitrant polluter, information about the cost of alternative technologies; and these devices are used to gather, from a very large number of other citizens who are adversely affected by the pollution, information about the costs of present pollution levels, which is the same thing as the value of having lower pollution levels. The advantage of the class action technique and the effluent tax technique is that they represent much less costly methods of assembling all this relevant information in the mind of a single decision-maker.

Consider how the class action technique works out. It will work best in circumstances where the number of people harmed by the pollution is not too large and each of them is harmed to a substantial degree. Suppose by statute we create, on behalf of persons thus damaged, an enforceable legal claim to compensation against the polluter. Those persons now have a substantial incentive to come forward, to band together in a single damage action against the polluter, and to develop in the courtroom the information which is uniquely within their possession as to the manner and extent of the harm that is being caused to them per month, or per some other unit of time. Those damages are the value of the environmental resource in its alternative uses, for example, the value of quietness as a residential amenity. The resulting award of damages imposes these costs, whatever they are, upon the polluter. It is not necessary for the court to go into the very difficult question of alternative technologies available to the polluter—we leave to him the question whether it would be wise to adopt alternative technologies. Since the system has the consequence of imposing the costs of pollution on the polluter, he now has strong incentives to spend up to, but no more than, 99 cents on pollution-reducing techniques in any unit of time if the result will be to reduce the level of damage claims against him in that unit of time by at least a dollar. This is precisely the way we should want him to behave, and it is possible to get him to behave in that way without ever going through the difficult process of extracting from him all he knows about the alternative technologies by which his production process can be carried on.

In substance the class action for compensatory damages creates incentives, on the part of precisely those people who have firsthand access to the information necessary for decision, to use the information to their own advantage. From the standpoint of the polluter we have made it profitable to attain the lowest practicable pollution level. The polluter now has the same incentives with respect to clean air or clean water that he has with respect to any other resource that he consumes.

We do not find it necessary to hold elaborate hearings and to issue detailed orders to steel manufacturers telling them how to run their plants so as to get the largest amount of steel out of the smallest amount of iron ore. They have to buy their iron ore, and they are only too happy to spend x dollars on an improved blast furnace if doing so will reduce their payments for iron ore by $x + 1$ dollars. Where the class action can be used, it achieves the same incentives and the same behavior as would a properly functioning market system. For the same reasons I spelled out in the context of aircraft noise, the law must provide that only damages and not injunctions can be awarded in such suits, and that only past and not future damages can be awarded. Periodic suits for past damages are contemplated.

A class action in which the polluter—the physical

emitter of effluent is liable for all harm caused by the effluent has one disadvantage, however: it ignores the possibility that the "victim" may be able, to some degree, to avoid harm to himself by modifying his own behavior. For example, in the case of airport noise, it might be true in a given situation that loss of $1 worth of residential values could be avoided either by installing 95c worth of noise surpressor on the airplane or by installing 90c worth of soundproofing on the residence. The latter course should be taken, but the homeowner has no incentive to insulate if the $1 loss will be compensated for by the airport: the investment would reduce his loss and his compensation by the same amount and yield him no benefit. Where very large numbers of victims are each harmed only slightly, this disadvantage is likely to be insignificant for sensible countermeasures are likely unavailable. But more typically correct incentives for both polluters and victims will be obtained only if polluters are allowed to avoid liability for harm to the degree harm could have been avoided more cheaply by victims than by polluters. And allowing such a defense to polluters greatly complicates the class-action and reduces its utility as a solution.

An effluent tax approach works in very much the same way as a class action one but never suffers from the disadvantage of dulling victims' incentives for self-protection. The tax is not paid to the victim, and he retains his natural incentive to protect himself from the consequences of those residual pollution levels that prevail after the polluter has made all desirable changes in his activities. Under the effluent tax approach government officials assemble information regarding the harms caused by specific pollution substances. For example, the government officials might investigate conditions in a specific river basin, conclude that about a ton of phosphates a week was being discharged into the river system by various enterprises bordering on the system, and that this particular pollutant was causing damage in the amount of $20,000 each week to other firms and individuals in the river basin. It would then level an excise tax in the amount of $10 a pound—$20,000 harm divided by 2,000 pounds of effluent—on the discharge of this chemical into the water system. It would make similar calculations with respect to each of the other important pollutants in the river system. Each enterprise along the river system would then be required to monitor its own operations and to pay over to the government a tax in the amount of $10 for every pound of phosphate that it discharged. Unannounced spot checks could be made on the operations of different companies from time to time to ensure that their reporting was honest, much the same way we make spot checks on our self-reporting system for income taxes.

This system, too, would create basically the correct set of incentives for polluters to achieve lower pollution levels, through whatever technologies were currently practicable, in their operations. They would make operating expenditures in order to reduce their tax burden. Different firms and industries would respond in different ways and to different degrees, but this is what we should desire. Some firms would find that with relatively small preemptions of alternative resources it would be possible for them to reduce their phosphate discharge to almost nothing, and they could thereby reduce their tax burden almost to zero. Other firms would find that there was very little they could do to modify their production techniques; their pollutant discharges and their tax burdens would remain comparatively high. The consequences would be that the price of their products would have to be increased, less of them would be consumed at those high prices, and the aggregate extent of operation of these industries would be contracted, leading to some diminution of pollution by that route.

With the passage of time we would gradually approach what I have referred to as an optimum level of pollution. To reduce pollution still further by an amount that would yield a dollar's worth of satisfactions in cleaner water, it would be necessary to preempt other resources that were yielding more than a dollar's worth of human satisfactions in their alternative occupations. To take that next step would be an error in my judgment. It amounts to treating clean water as an end in itself rather than as one of a variety of contributors to human satisfactions—rather than as a means to achieving the largest amount of human satisfactions.

Now that I have sketched out the general pattern

of how an effluent tax system might work, let me go back and be more precise about several points which I left ambiguous in the interest of presenting a general picture. As I said, the effluent tax and class action approaches eliminate only one of two parts of the information-gathering problem. It is still necessary officially to gather information about the harms caused by the effluents. It is not necessary to gather information about the present and alternative technologies of the polluters. But, it does not follow that because we have eliminated only one of the two parts of the problem, we have made only a 50 percent improvement on the tailormade-order approach. For the information-gathering process about present and alternative technologies of the polluter, in my opinion, represents a more difficult part of the information assembly problem than does gathering information about harms. Neither part will be easy or precise. However, it is the polluters who have incentives to be recalcitrant under the tailormade-order approach, to slow the process down, to give us only that information which we can extract from them by coercive legal techniques. In contrast, those who are harmed have incentives to cooperate with the system. The one part of the information-gathering problem that we have eliminated is, I think, the more difficult part.

Second, let me make briefly an important but fairly technical point. Computed as I have suggested, the level of effluent taxes would not be precisely correct. If set as I have suggested, effluent taxes would correspond in amount to the average level of harm done by one unit of a particular effluent. Theoretically, the correct level of the tax should be the marginal amount of harm done by the last unit of that particular effluent introduced into the water system. One cannot generalize about the extent to which the average would differ from the marginal rate of harm; in some instances the difference would be trivial, in other substantial. In most cases I would expect taxes based on marginal rates of harm to be somewhat higher than taxes based on average rates. However, it would be far more difficult to administer a system based on marginal rates, and it would be more difficult for most people to understand what was going on, so a marginal system would be more difficult to achieve politically. Since all of the calaculations that will be involved in such a system will be less than perfectly precise, I would be delighted to settle for a carefully constructed system of effluent taxes based on average harm rates. In any event, this same average versus marginal difficulty inheres in the tailormade-order approach. That system just happens to be so much less precise that the average versus marginal distinction I am noting here does not emerge there with any analytical clarity; it is present nevertheless.

To me one of the most disturbing features about the ecology movement is the totally irrational response that many environmental enthusiasts give to effluent tax proposals. Such proposals are brushed aside with the cavalier observation that they consititute a "license to pollute." If such comments have any intellectual, as opposed to emotional, content at all, they can only suggest that the speaker has in mind some alternative system of control that would result in a zero pollution rate—a system under which all firms would really stop polluting rather than merely reduce the level of effluence. And there is no such system. The tailormade-order approach, toward which we seem to be drifting in this country, confers a much more pernicious license to continue pollution. For no such order will direct measures that will reduce pollution levels to zero, but rather to some level which some government official finds practicable and economically feasible. Until confronted with a tailormade order, the firm has no incentive to reduce pollution. Once the firm has complied with that order and attained that level of pollution, whatever it is, it has no incentive whatsoever to improve on its performance. It pays nothing for the air or water resource that it consumes by polluting at that level. It has no incentive to find improvements in the technology of its processes. So, judged by the end result as well as by the consideration that costs of administration would be substantially lower, I find the effluent tax approach far superior to the tailormade-order approach.

Why Does Tailormade Persist?

In view of these considerations one must ask with some bewilderment why it is that our legislatures have tended so persistently toward a tailormade-order approach rather than toward the use of either class actions or effluent taxes. I have only the most baseless of speculations to offer in response to this question. For what they are worth, here are several.

Historically, we have used taxes to raise revenue rather than to alter behavior. When one's purpose is to raise revenue, then a tax should be levied upon some activity which will not diminish because it is taxed. We tax income, for example, precisely because people have very little alternative but to earn income, despite the tax. In economic terms, it is a desirable characteristic of a revenue-producing tax that it be "allocatively neutral." In the environmental context, of course, our purpose is precisely the opposite. We choose to levy a tax because we do want the effluent on which the tax is levied to go away to some considerable extent. Our hope is that the tax device will raise as little revenue as possible. Perhaps this is such an unaccustomed and strange set of tax concepts that legislators simply have not become acclimated to them.

Alternatively, one could offer rather cynical explanations. Politicians have a bias for increasing the size of their staffs, and far more employees are needed to administer the tailor-made order approach. One might suggest that effluent taxes are not used precisely because they would be effective, that the "vested interests" have succeeded in blocking precisely those measures which would have the consequences we desire. This view rests on a "bad-man" conspiracy view of the world, and in my experience explanations having to do with ignorance and cultural rigidity and habit are far more often correct than conspiracy explanations.

On the other hand, there is no doubt that many large industrial organizations are very nervous about the environmental movement. They are troubled by uncertainty about how it will affect them and their competitors. If they could be sure that the costs imposed on their competitors would be as great as those imposed upon themselves, they would rest easier, but there can be no assurance that that will be the case under a well-devised scheme. Under our present market system, companies located themselves near cheap supplies of the resources for which they had to pay, but they did not accord much significance to environmental factors in deciding where to situate their plants—precisely because they did not plan to pay for the environmental resources they consumed. When we start accounting for environmental resources, it is likely to be the case that Company A will be hit much harder by effluent taxes than Company B precisely because Company A is consuming larger quantities of those resources. The same thing is true of a correctly administered system of tailormade commands, for it, too, should be cost-based, and the imposition of a competitive disadvantage should not be regarded as indicating "economic infeasibility." But I confidently predict that the opposite view will prevail under that system. So perhaps in this context the "bad-man" theory cannot be dismissed entirely.

The explanation I find most plausible rests on two factors. One is that most legislators have not carefully thought through environmental problems in any very analytical way. When someone proposes an effluent tax system to them, all the horrendous imponderables involved in such a system leap to their minds. How, they ask, will we ever decide the level at which such taxes should be set? What they do not seem to realize is that the process of issuing tailormade orders to individual companies as to how they are to modify their activities is dependent on precisely the same amount and same items of information. They do not seem to realize that the consequences of being a little wrong or very wrong in issuing orders of that kind are every bit as serious, both for the company and for the community as a whole, as are the consequences of being a little or very wrong in setting effluent tax levels. There is a delusive simplicity about telling people what to do.

Second, effluent tax systems would necessarily require that the legislature delegate to administrative bodies the power to set effluent tax levels. Those tax levels will have to differ from river basin to river basin, or from air shed to air shed, just as specific orders have to be tailored to the different situations involved. Congress, and state legislatures as well, historically have been very reluctant to delegate the authority to levy taxes. The power to tax is seen as an enormously powerful and potentially destructive power that must be closely guarded. The power to tax is indeed the power to destroy, but so also is the power to issue orders. Perhaps what we should find surprising is not that there is legislative reluctance to delegate taxing authority, but that there is so little legislative reluctance to delegate the equally destructive authority to tell individual companies how they must modify their operations.

Whatever the explanation is, in my judgment we must overcome the political and institutional barriers. The effluent tax approach holds out far greater promise for coping with our environmental problems than do the approaches now regarded as traditional.

In the years to come, the United States is going to be badly divided politically. Viewed in the aggregate, ours is not an affluent society. Too large a proportion of our population is badly in need of more of our traditional goods and services, such as food, housing, education, transportation, and medical care. Our present approaches to the ecology problem, because they are so much more inefficient and wasteful of resources then they need be, will raise the prices and restrict the supply of these traditional items. It will come into sharp conflict with the demands of the low-income groups. If ecology problems are attacked properly, the result will be that we will have a larger aggregate quantity of satisfactions to distribute as we will among our population, and the conflict, while still present, will be diminished. Therefore, it seems to me that the most serious challenge is to find government techniques that conserve our environmental resources with the least possible sacrifice in the productive efficiency of our economy. The panoply of threats that confront our environmental resources are, at last, receiving adequate public attention. The question of control techniques continues to be very much neglected.

5

Interregional Problems in Implementing an Effluent Tax System

This chapter will sketch out a process to implement the attainment of optimum levels of pollution, first and briefly, as it might be executed within a single sovereignty; then, as extrapolated to the international level, with emphasis on the complications introduced by the multi-sovereign character of that level.

Both for national and for international purposes, the total set of polluting activities can usefully be broken down into two subcategories: 1) the episodic polluting accident, and 2) the continuous polluting process. These two categories can be illustrated with examples. A maritime collision by an oil tanker with resultant spillage of petroleum belongs to the first category; the more or less continuous discharge into the atmosphere of hydrocarbons and oxides of nitrogen from internal-combustion engines in transportation vehicles belongs to the second. The purpose in pointing out these two categories is to separate a category of historically discrete events which might conceivably be handled one at a time and which are in some acknowledged sense malfunctions, from a second category of more or less continuous processes of a socially useful kind which must, as a practical matter, be acknowledged as processes and with respect to which our emphasis must be either on altering the characteristics of the process or curtailing the extent to which it is utilized.

Where episodic accidents are concerned, in either a domestic or an international context, results reasonably approximating the optimum can be obtained by machinery virtually identical to our present-day court systems simply by imposing upon the activity that caused the accident the full range of social costs that were caused by the accident. There will be problems, of course—problems of obtaining jurisdiction over the parties, problems of substantive liability and defenses, for example. As to the substantive questions, it is fairly clear from existent scholarship that best results are obtained by imposing liability without any showing of fault upon the activity that gave rise to the accident and by making available, as a defense to that activity, immunity only with respect to those particular claimants as to whom the defendant can show a failure to take reasonable protective measures that were within their knowledge and command.

I intend for the most part to address myself to the continuous pollution processes because the problems posed by continuous processes are more difficult to solve, nationally or internationally. I shall first sketch a crude outline of a system for national control of continuous pollution processes and then attempt to extrapolate to the international context.

National Implementation

Calculating Tax Rates

Functionally there are two principal tasks to be performed in implementing a system of effluent taxation at the national level. The first task is to determine the tax rate per unit of effluent discharged into the environment. This is essentially a two-step process. The first step is to determine, and to place a dollar value on, the aggregate amount of harm being caused by a particular effluent, for example, oxides of nitrogen. It must be stressed here that this same estimate is made explicitly or implicitly under any control system. It is now being done implicitly. Under the system proposed here, harm to property would be measured by diminution in market value. Harm to persons would be determined by estimation of components (health, recreation, etc.) through the political process. Unlike the present system, the estimations of harm would be made consciously, explicitly, and subject to public scrutiny and discussion. The second step is to determine the aggregate quantity, in moles or pounds or tons, of the effluent currently being discharged by all processes into the environment. From these two figures an average dollar amount of harm per unit of effluent can be calculated, and this number becomes the basic effluent tax rate for that particular chemical. The second major task is to monitor the various processes which introduce this effluent into the environment and to impose on them a tax per unit of effluent discharged in the amount of the tax rate.

The average charge per unit of effluent is not the theoretical correct tax: theoretically, every unit of effluent being discharged into the environment should be taxed at a rate which corresponds to the amount of harm done by the last unit of effluent discharged into the environment; or, put somewhat differently, each unit should be taxed in the amount of harm that could be avoided if one less unit was discharged into the environment. In short, the tax rate should be the marginal harm rate rather than the average harm rate, but marginal harm rates are far more difficult to calculate than average harm rates, and average rates probably should be used as a reasonable approximation. In theory, again, one cannot be certain whether the average rates are above or below the marginal rates, hence we cannot be certain whether the tax is somewhat too high or too low but, in the majority of instances, the average harm rate will be less than the marginal harm rate and hence the taxes will be somewhat too low. (As can be seen from the graph, where pollution is relatively low [far lower than saturation levels of concentration], the average rate is lower than the marginal rate of harm being caused. This relatively low level of pollution is probably the empirical reality in the great majority of instances in the United States.) Since the several determinations involved in these calculations will involve substantial ranges of uncertainty, it would be appropriate to select an average harm rate that is in the upper end of the uncertainty range so as to err in the direction of the marginal rate.

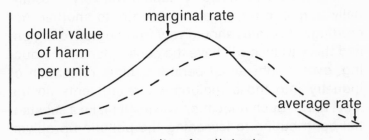

units of pollutant

Once the rates to be applied are determined, self-monitoring and reporting can be required of all substantial industrial and municipal contributors. Random checks could then be made on the accuracy of their monitoring and reporting processes. In short, this portion of the system could be operated very much as our present federal income tax system is administered. With the exception of privately owned automobiles and trucks, this self-reporting system could cover the vast preponderance of pollution contributors. As to privately owned internal-combustion vehicles, an officially administered monitoring and assessment system would certainly have to be used; however, this does not seem relevant in the international context and so I will attempt no further description of such a system here.

Establishing a System of Regional Taxation

In a large nation such as the United States, the harm rates for particular effluents will vary substantially from one region of the country to another. Accordingly, tax rates should vary from region to region, and this variance will have the consequence of inducing, over a substantial period of time, relocation of industry into those regions where effluents do the least harm. Such relocation will itself make a substantial contribution to lessening the pollution problem, and pains should be taken to assure that the tax system conduces to that result. Accordingly, it would be a serious error to establish uniform tax rates for the nation as a whole, for that would eliminate incentives for relocation. Thus, although the general principles and characteristics of the effluent tax system should be established nationally, the harm rate determinations should be conducted on a regional basis, and the tax rates should vary region by region.

The regions should be drawn to correspond to areas within which the harm caused by a unit of particular effluent is more or less homogeneous. It follows that the regions should be drawn to correspond roughly to meteorological airsheds and to river-basin systems, and that the regions appropriate for air pollution problems may not be the regions appropriate for water pollution problems.

An Industry Response—Relocation

Assume that the system described is put into operation, and consider the reaction of industries in the years that follow. Historically industries have located themselves so as to minimize their costs of assembling their production inputs and of distributing their production outputs to the customer markets. They have done this without taking into account the social cost of an important category of resources they consume —namely, those environmental resources which are owned in common by the community and for which no payment has heretofore been required. After the system is put into effect, payment will be required for these resources, and many companies will correctly conclude that their geographic location is not optimum when these new payment obligations are taken into account. Hence, we can expect a transition period following implementation of any effective environmental measures, during which considerable industry relocation will occur. Not all firms will move at once, of course. To the extent they have sunk investments in immobile plant and equipment, they will stay where they are, even at the cost of paying higher taxes than would be necessary elsewhere, while those sunk investments are exhausted and amortized. But when the time for reinvestment in immobile assests approaches, their investment will be made at geographic locations perceived to be optimum in view of effluent tax rate differentials as well as the level of other factor costs.

The inevitability of this transitional period of relocation is by no means unique to an effluent tax system. It would occur either to a greater or smaller extent under a system which involved the imposition of standards, and the more nearly optimum the standards were—that is, the more nearly they minimized social cost—the more nearly the extent and character of relocation would approximate that which would occur under an effluent tax system.

The fact that there will be such a transitional relocation period has two important implications. First, a widespread pattern of relocation of this type will itself have social costs: it will result in temporary unemployment at some locations when industries move away, high wage rates at new locations to which industries move where there is not a resident work force of appropriate size and composition, and an eventual redistribution of the working population to correspond to new production locations. It is desirable that this relocation phenomenon not occur too rapidly, and to that end it probably would be wise to introduce the tax system gradually. The best way to do this is to compute the tax rates as precisely as possible and announce the eventual tax rate that is expected to prevail in the region at the end of the transition period. But polluters should then be required to pay, for example, only 10 percent of the tax in the first year, 20 percent of the tax in the second year, and so on. This approach would facilitate industry consideration of optimum relocation points as early as possible, would enable the process of relocation to start as soon as possible but on a gradual basis, and would tend to minimize the impact of relocation costs by distributing them over a significant time horizon.

The relocation phenomenon, in addition to arguing for a graduated introduction of the taxes, is relevant to the political composition of the regional entities that make the rate-of-harm determinations for each region. Regions where pollution costs are apparently highest will tend to become net exporters of polluting industrial activities, and regions where harm rates are lowest will tend to be net importers of such activities during the transition period. It is predictable that, if the regional authorities are political representatives only of the region, there would be a uniform tendency to estimate harm rates and set taxes at the lowest defensible level. At first blush, this prediction may seem false, or at least paradoxical; but it can be made with some confidence. The phenomenon that will be involved in precisely the classic phenomenon of protecting local industry that we observe in international trade. Such protectionist measures always involve the imposition of indirect and usually non-obvious costs on the resident population; indeed it is the desirability of eliminating those hidden costs which is the philosophical and economic basis that underlies the argument for free international trade. Nonetheless it will prove to be true in the pollution tax context, as in the international trade context, that regional authorities would rather incur continued high pollution costs than face up to the local unemployment and relocation costs that would attend a more nearly rational costing system. It follows, at least in a national system, that the regional authorities should not merely be representative of the regional population but of the nation as a whole, to assure that harm rates are not assessed at unrealistically low levels. It is less clear than an analogous conclusion follows with respect to the international situation.

The International Context

Allocating Tax Revenues

In the national context effluent taxes would be paid into the federal treasury. In the international context, the issue of to whom the tax revenues would be paid is obviously far more controversial. It is critical to recognize in either context that the success of the system does not depend upon who receives the tax revenues. It is important only that the social costs of the environmental resources preempted by any activity be imposed on that activity; what is done with the tax revenues that correspond to those costs, while politically important, is nearly irrelevant for the attainment of an optimum level of pollution. So long as the revenues are not used in ways that are counterproductive to the environmental effort, for example, to subsidize the local industries that were required to pay the taxes in the first instance, only an issue of income distribution is posed by tax revenue distributions. Recognition of this point is important, because it will enable the top administering entity to use the tax revenues to compensate, in ways that are not counterproductive, those populations which tend to suffer the highest relocation costs and thus to minimize initial resistance to introduction of the system.

The Sovereignty-Standing Issue

A second and more complex issue comes sharply into focus in the international context which, although theoretically present in the national context as well, is of far less practical importance there. For reasons that will become more apparent hereafter, it can be called the sovereignty-standing issue. It is both complex and elusive, so it is best to proceed first by way of example.

Assume the existence of a geographically isolated

nation, N, perhaps a large mid-Pacific island, somewhat analogous to Australia, which has a two-commodity gross national product—bread and clothing. Its bread-producing processes preempt no scarce resource that is not adequately accounted for in well-functioning competitive markets—that is to say, it is not a polluting activity. Its clothing-manufacturing processes, on the contrary, cause large quantities of nitrous oxide to be discharged into its atmosphere, and its population's health is injured thereby. N has adopted no system, or perhaps an inadequate system, of pollution control, and hence the full social costs of its effluent production are not imposed on the clothing-manufacture process. As a consequence, too large a proportion of N's labor, capital, and natural resources is devoted to clothing manufacture and too small a proportion to food manufacture. That is to say, its population in the aggregate would be better off if more food and less clothing were produced, a consequence that would follow from the imposition of appropriate effluent taxes on the clothing-manufacture process. However, no one other than the citizenry of N is prejudiced by this social structure; for one reason or another all the nitrous oxide is either precipitated on the landmass of N or chemically converted in its immediate atmosphere into harmless constitutents.

A persuasive argument can be made that the problem is not one of international concern. I decline to state international indifference in more categorical terms, because it is entirely possible that this local malorganization does have some international trade impacts. It is likely for example,that N is a significant exporter of clothing and perhaps an importer of food, although those trade patterns do not in fact correspond to the situation of true comparative advantage. It would be accurate to say that N is subsidizing its clothing exports by means of a hidden domestic excise tax on its food production, and in an ideal world such practices would not be permitted. But I would argue, nonetheless, that this should be regarded as a problem of international trade and ignored in the context of international pollution control although, as the foregoing example indicates, the two problems are by no means independent.

Let me now alter the example by assuming that two separate sovereignties, nations N_1 and N_2, are situated on a mid-Pacific landmass. The situation in N_1 is as described in the preceding paragraphs. N_2 has a similar two-product GNP of food and clothing; but because its resource characteristics differ, different production processes are used, with the consequence that food production yields the untaxed effluent, nitrous oxide, and clothing manufacture pays its full social cost. The effluent from N_1 impairs health in both N_1 and N_2, and so also does the effluent from N_2; but again, there are no effects on populations off the landmass except for the failure of international trade to reflect the true comparative advantage. Whether the larger international community should now regard the situation as a matter of its concern is a more difficult question. Again, it seems clear that international intervention on the grounds of the trade effect should be left to international trade organizations, and international environmental organizations should intervene, if at all, only on some other basis.

This hypothetical situation can be altered one more time by assuming that the effluent discharge by the clothing-manufacture process in N_1 and the food-manufacture process in N_2 is instantaneously discharged throughout the entire air envelope of the globe, with the consequence that its adverse health characteristics impinge homogeneously upon the populations of all nations. It is now clear beyond doubt that the problem is appropriately regarded as one of international concern and that all populations have a valid claim to "equal representation" (whatever that is taken to mean in the international context) in the alleviation of the problem.

Pollution Optimization in an
International Context—Three Approaches

Using these slim examples for illumination, let me return to a higher level of abstraction. The sovereignty-standing problems I have suggested in the foregoing paragraphs are presented by the issue of international environmental control regardless of whether one contemplates as his operative instrument the setting of effluent standards implemented by tailor-made orders or contemplates the use of effluent taxation: the case for international imposition of standards on the industry of country N in the first example is neither stronger nor weaker than the case for the imposition of taxation.

It should be clear, moreover, that if every nation were to adopt for domestic purposes an effective system of environmental control through effluent tax measures such as those I have suggested for a single sovereignty, and were to take into account, in making its harm determinations, the adverse effects that effluents had on other populations as well as upon its own, an optimum world solution would result. There would be no need to treat the problem of international controls separately. That approach would also have the consequence of effectuating the principle of comparative advantage in international trade. Hence, one international approach to the environmental problem would be to seek adoption by each nation, for internal purposes, of such an effluent tax system. Such an approach will, no doubt, be regarded by most as hopelessly utopian.

A second solution would be to impose effluent taxes on the gross *exports* of effluents by each nation, in accordance with a harm rate determined with respect to the meteorological airshed or water system throughout which those exports caused harm. This approach would imply, in my second example, that nation N_1 would be required, as a nation, to pay effluent taxes on its exports of nitrous oxide into N_2, and that N_2 would be required to pay taxes for its exports of that same effluent into N_1. Representation on the administering body would not be limited to the nations within the adversely affected environmental region; and these two nations would not be free to ignore one another's pollution exports, tacitly or explicitly. Again it must be emphasized that the nature and redistribution of the fund into which those taxes are paid is a matter of indifference so far as the environmental problem itself is concerned, but the fund must not be redistributed in a way that undermines tax incentives, as would, for example, redistribution in proportion to initial payments.

An important distinction to be noted between the first and second taxation approaches suggested is that, under the second approach, the tax would be imposed upon nation N_1 and not upon the individual clothing manufacturers of N_1 in accordance with their individual production of the effluent. Accordingly, a private incentive on the part of the individual clothing manufacturers in N_1 to alter their industrial processes to reduce effluent levels to an optimum would be created if and only if nation N_1 were to pass on the costs of its international tax obligation to those industries, scaled in proportion to their individual contributions. Alternatively, N_1 might attempt to alter behavior of the manufacturers by imposing effluent standards upon them. A failure by N_1 to take either step would be, in substance, a determination to continue subsidizing its clothing industry not only to the extent that it was theretofore subsidizing it (in the amount of the social costs imposed by the industry on its own nationals) but to increase the subsidy by an amount corresponding to the social cost that the effluents were imposing upon the peoples of other nations. In order thus to increase those subsidies, it would be necessary for N_1 to levy a heavier tax burden domestically so as to raise the funds necessary to make payments to the designated international fund. This approach would certainly strengthen the incentives of each nation to optimize its pollution levels, at least insofar as they had extranational impact, but it would not compel them to do so.

A third international approach would, again, require demarcation of regions, corresponding to natural meteorological airsheds, international riverbasin systems, and other international water systems, but under this approach the control body with jurisdiction over the region would represent only those nations within the designated region. Depending on the characteristics of the effluent involved, some of these bodies would be worldwide, and representation on them would be correspondingly broad. Others might embrace as few as two nations, and representation would be confined to those nations. The important implication of the limited concept of political representation embodied in this third appraoch is that the resulting regional autonomy would permit some control groups to adopt vigorous measures approximating optimum solution and permit others to exhibit greater laxity. For example, in each case the regional body would have the authority to determine for its region not only the appropriate harm rate and the corresponding per unit effluents tax, but also how rapidly the tax would be imposed in full measure in view of local transitional problems. Authority could be delegated to each regional body to decide whether the tax would be imposed on individual industries within member nations in accordance with the individual industry's contribution to effluent levels. And finally, with reference to my hypothetical Pacific landmass consisting of N_1 and N_2, this third approach would allow the regional body for air pollution control, on which only N_1 and N_2 would be represented, simply to ignore the entire problem of nitrous oxide if it wished.

An International Pollution Control System—Its Function and Structure

Data Assembly

A desirable first step toward implementation of an international control system might be the creation of an international body with worldwide responsibility for fact-gathering and dissemination. There are several types of information to be assembled. First, data must be obtained on the ways, and the extent to which, our air envelope and our international waters are being altered in their composition by the productive processes of civilization. Second, it should be determined which of these materials cause harm, either directly to man because he assimilates them from his environment, or indirectly in that they make other resources less readily usable by him—for example, injury by chemical discharges to fish life or to timber stands. Thrid, information should be assembled on the patterns of dissemination of harmful pollutants. From what is known of the situation in the United States, there is reason to believe that most pollutants do not migrate worldwide but, in very preponderant proportion, remain in the airshed or water system of their origin. Finally, attempts should be made at quantification, in units of account, of the harm caused by a half-dozen important pollutants. These studies should be made both in highly developed and urbanized areas and also in underdeveloped societies, for harm rates may prove to differ substantially with different development levels.

As for the technique of data assembly, insofar as possible this should be done by the collection and standardization of data currently being generated by various national monitoring bodies. Insofar as these national efforts fail to yield needed data, then the international agency should engage in direct monitoring activities needed to produce that information.

Pollution Control

At a subsequent point in time, when more information is available, transition from information-gathering to polution control would be expected. For purposes of control there should be one entity, worldwide both in its responsiblity and its representation, and there should also be a fairly large number of regional organizations drawn to correspond geographically to principal airsheds and water system. The worldwide organization would probably have certain coordination responsibilities with respect to regional organizations, and it would also have direct responsibility for control of those harmful pollutants which exhibit worldwide dissemination characteristics. The regional organizations would have responsibility for pollutants that originated in and were disseminated, in major part, within their respective regions. The regional organization should have a high degree of autonomy, if not with respect to the methods employed, at least with respect to the magnitude of incentive taxes imposed.

Each entity, whether regional or worldwide, would make harm rate determinations for the geographic area of its responsibility. Ideally, it would then impose, with respect to each effluent, directly on each contributing activity within its sphere, an effluent tax that corresponded to the average harm rate. However, it seems quite unlikely that, as an international community, we are ready for such direct intervention in internal affairs by an international organization. Accordingly, I think it would be more realistic to imagine a system in which the international organization imposed on each member nation an aggregated tax equivalent to the sum of effluent taxes corresponding to the pollutant exports of that particular country.
The type of structure described is compatible with the

assumption that one nation has no standing to participate in the determination of appropriate levels of pen-
alty or control over the production processes of a
second nation unless the first is within the area of
impact to which the pollutants of that second nation
extend. I will try to explain why I think this view of the
standing question is the most tenable and operational
one. In many instances, perhaps in the great majority
of instances, the regional control bodies will embrace
nations which are more or less homogeneous with
regard to their standard of living and state of technological advancement. Where this is true, the problem will be much simpler than where it is not.

Very substantial additional political difficulty will
be introduced into the problem of pollution control
wherever significant income variances are found
within a region over which a unified control program
is being attempted. A fact that simply must be recognized by environmental enthusiasts is that environmental amenities, even if one is talking about
controlling pollutants which impair health and shorten
lifespan, fall in the category of a luxury good. Any
attempt to produce steel, or to provide transportation,
or even to grow crops, without introducing harmful
materials into the environment, will significantly reduce the quantity of steel or transportation or crops
that can be produced with a given amount of resources.
This is merely to say that pollution control is an expensive proposition.

The hard fact is that to produce the steel without

producing large quantities of sulfides of hydrogen, for example, one must divert, from the production of other useful goods and services in the society, a large number of highly skilled personnel and a wide variety of other natural resources which, but for the pollution control effort, would have flowed instead into the production of traditional goods and services. A society that decides to enjoy substantially cleaner air and purer water has decided, in substance, to reallocate its scarce natural resources to produce cleaner air and purer water, and less housing and food and steel and transportation and medical care. And it is in terms of sacrifice of those alternative consumer goods and services that the costs of pollution control are best measured.

In a technologically advanced and comparatively affluent nation such as the United States, such a program nevertheless makes obvious sense, if not carried too far. In a society where the great majority of the population is functioning at a bare survival level, however, it is absurd to suggest that the well-being of its people would be advanced by reducing the production of food and shelter and medical care by 10 percent in order to have cleaner air and water. In short, the critical question in every nation is the rate of tradeoff between these two different types of consumption goods, and the sensible point of balance will be very different in comparatively affluent nations from that in comparatively impoverished ones.

The point may be more readily understandable if

stated as an inter-person, rather than as an inter-nation, proposition: It is inherent in the nature of most environmental amenities that all persons within the community must consume them in equal physical amounts—clean air or clean water cannot be provided for one citizen without providing it for all. They are what the economists call public goods. Moreover, existing information suggests that they will prove to be very expensive goods in terms of alternative use of resources. Comparatively affluent people would, if it were a matter of free individual choice, buy and consume these goods in much greater physical quantities than would their low-income counterparts. But the situation is worse than that: existing data indicate that these public goods are regarded as luxuries; and that they would be consumed by the affluent, under conditions of free individual choice, not merely in those greater absolute amounts proportionate to the larger incomes of the affluent, but that the affluent would devote to them greater proportions of income as well. In short, high-income groups not only would spend more dollars but would spend a larger proportion of their larger budgets on these amenities than the proportion that would be spent by lower-income groups of their smaller budgets.

A country that launches upon a vigorous pollution control program (and it makes no difference in this regard whether it uses an effluent tax appraoch or a standards approach) has implicitly decided to finance the production of luxury goods by a hidden excise tax upon such staples as food and housing that at least some parts of its population regard as essential to bare survival. In my judgment it will prove to be politically inevitable, in any society that attempts to pursue vigorous and pervasive pollution control activities, that it simultaneously adopt a variety of other measures intended to redistribute income in order to offset an income redistribution from poor to rich that would otherwise be the implicit result of pollution control efforts.

These same poor-to-rich income redistribution consequences will occur between nations under any rigidly uniform international pollution control scheme. It follows from all this that an international control entity with responsibility for a region composed of underdeveloped countries will, quite correctly from the standpoint of its own populations, impose far less severe deterrents on polluting activities than would be appropriate in a region composed of more affluent nations. If, in the international context, regions are formed which are more geographically encompassing than they need be, and rich and poor nations are brought together within the confines of a single such organization, then they will face the political necessity of compromising on penalties that are inappropriately low from the standpoint of the wealthier ones. This very difficult political problem should be avoided to the extent possible. If these two groups of peoples are not in the same airshed—if it is not atmospherically inevitable that they breathe air of the same level of

purity—then it is absurd to face all the political problems implicit in insisting that they do so. After all, they
do not consume food in the same quantities or enjoy
shelter of the same characteristics or medical care of
the same quality. Different levels of atmospheric purity
will be appropriate to their situations and would be
chosen by them if choice were possible.

It is for this reason that I have suggested a comparatively narrow view of what nations have standing
to participate in the determinations that must be made
as part of any control system, and have insisted that
the regional approach be taken with regions being
drawn as narrowly as geophysical circumstances
permit.

Two further comments which bear on this
income-distribution aspect of the pollution problem
are appropriate here. First, because low-income regions will impose and should impose less severe
penalties on their productive activities, they will come
to enjoy a comparative advantage in trade. If compen-
sating tariff barriers are not erected by more affluent
nations, we should expect that appropriate pollution
controls in each nation would tend to shift a larger
fraction of manufacturing (and polluting) activities to
the less developed countries. Most would find this an
encouraging prospect, but no doubt it will be assailed
in some quarters as a new form of imperialism.

Second and finally, I must point out again that a
stream of receipts will be generated by the effluent tax
approach. As I have said, it is not critical to the success

of the pollution control endeavor what is done with these receipts. But it should be fairly obvious that they may be germane to the situation in a slightly different way: one of the most important uses of those receipts may prove to be the offsetting of perverse income redistribution effects that would otherwise attend pollution control.